MW01178207

A Rooted Mind

Saying yes to beauty, wellness and
deeply-rooted mental health

Beth Gager

BALBOA.
PRESS

A DIVISION OF HAY HOUSE

Balboa Press books may be ordered through booksellers or by contacting:

Balboa Press
A Division of Hay House
1663 Liberty Drive
Bloomington, IN 47403
www.balboapress.com
1 (877) 407-4847

Because of the dynamic nature of the Internet, any web addresses or
links contained in this book may have changed since publication and
may no longer be valid. The views expressed in this work are solely those
of the author and do not necessarily reflect the views of the publisher,
and the publisher hereby disclaims any responsibility for them.

The author of this book does not dispense medical advice or prescribe the use
of any technique as a form of treatment for physical, emotional, or medical
problems without the advice of a physician, either directly or indirectly. The
intent of the author is only to offer information of a general nature to help
you in your quest for emotional and spiritual well-being. In the event you use
any of the information in this book for yourself, which is your constitutional
right, the author and the publisher assume no responsibility for your actions.

Any people depicted in stock imagery provided by Thinkstock are models,
and such images are being used for illustrative purposes only.
Certain stock imagery © Thinkstock.

Printed in the United States of America.

ISBN: 978-1-4525-2001-8 (sc)
ISBN: 978-1-4525-2002-5 (hc)
ISBN: 978-1-4525-2003-2 (e)

Library of Congress Control Number: 2014914161
Balboa Press rev. date: 08/15/2014

For Laura, who has walked with me every step
of the way and now has the wings to fly.
And for Malaina, my beautiful writing angel.

Contents

INTRODUCTION

I write this book to you with a purpose in my heart. My purpose is to show you your own magnificence. I have come far to be in this place where I stand in front of you, where I can look you straight in your eyes and see your brilliance gazing back at me. I have been where I never imagined I would go. I have been to the place that the world calls mental illness. And I have come back. I have discovered my own self as a healer, and I have come to see all of us who go to this place called mental illness as the healers that we are. So many of us struggle there for so long that we have a hard time coming back. We don't know who we are inside or what we are coming back to. The world sees us as broken, and that is what we become.

Maybe you are one of the ones who are still struggling. If so, then this book is for you. No matter how many times you have been lost, there is always a place for you to be found. I offer you a window into my heart, and I will show you the ways in which I found myself again after I had been where I seemed very, very lost. It is not as complicated as you might think. You already have everything you need inside of you to go exactly where you have always been meant to go. I hope that my words offer you a pathway and a glimpse into the brilliance of your own heart. I am not going to spend a lot of time talking about the hard places. But I honor that those places exist. I am aware that you have been hurt. I understand that your hurt goes deep. I have been to the hard places and the hurt places, too. But I have found a way to heal. I have found a way back into the beauty that lives all around us. Don't think that you are alone in the lost places. Don't think there is something so particularly broken about you that you can never be healed. Together we will discover who you are in the quiet place that lives inside of you. We will uncover the green shoots of your soul that have been buried under the muck. Together we will unearth the gems buried in your heart that call to you with their brightly colored beauty. You have those gems within you.

The world might see you as lost and broken. And maybe there is still a part of you in which that is true. But there is another part of you. That is the part of you that we need to talk about. The world is full of broken people, whether they are called mentally ill or not. You have so much more to do than stay broken. It is your right, your purpose, your gift to be whole. Your wholeness is shining from your heart into your eyes right now. Look in the mirror, and let yourself see it. Let yourself get a glimpse of who you are in the place where mental illness has never touched. You are in this world for a reason. You have a calling, something that is yours to do in the world. The rest of us need you. Take a deep breath, and let yourself be touched by the beating of your own heart. No matter where you have been before, take this chance to come right here, right now. Let go of who you are in the broken places, for just a second, just a breath, just a heartbeat. For this one moment in time, make a new beginning. You are who you are for a reason. You are beautiful and whole and full of light. You are so much more than what the world sees, more than what the world sees as mentally ill. This is the time for you to see yourself clearly. This is the moment when you decide to own your story and your life. You can be who you need to be for yourself and for everyone else that you touch. I believe in you. And I know the truth that is crying from your heart to be heard. Your heart is, right now and always, telling you the truth. You are here. You are alive. You are beautiful. And you are magnificent. My wish for you is that, by the time you get to the end of this book, you know that for yourself.

CHAPTER ONE

Broken

I am done with being broken. I am no longer interested in being wounded. For a very long time, I had to stay small to be who I needed to be in the world. But then being small stopped working. Hiding my most essential self beneath layers of fear and heaviness was no longer an option for me. I have always been brave. Throughout my whole life, I have done more than what was asked of me. When faced with a choice, I have always chosen the path with the most truth and light—even if it is full of fear and most often means I will face it alone. That, in fact, is what has led me here, to you. Here, where I am sharing my story with you, so you will have the same chances that I have had. I have had the opportunity to stop being broken. I have found the way to the place where we can give up on being wounded.

It doesn't happen in one day. You don't go from living your life enfolded in the fear and pain and trauma of the worst thing that ever happened to you to being a whole, vibrant person who is filled every day with awesome beauty and joy. It takes time. And you have to walk there. Step by step. This is the story of my long walk. It is the story of my journey from a time when I seemed to be very, very lost to the place where I stand now, where I feel completely found. When I look back, I see that the walk through the lost places wasn't really that long. Not when compared with all the joyful walking that I still have ahead of me. But the walk was hard, and my feet hurt. I had to lose everything that I held dear to be able to find it again. And that has made it dearer still.

I want to be clear that this is not a book about illness. It has nothing to do with what is wrong. This is a book about wellness and roots. It's a book about a journey that brings you back to the only place you ever need to be, which is inside of your truest self. This book will show you a way to come back to your clearest, most beautiful self. The self that you were always meant to be. This is a story about being big. About being grounded. About living with your roots so far in the ground that your branches are free to sway in the breeze unencumbered. This is a story about me, but it is also a story about you. You are magnificent. And it is time for you to realize that magnificence. What you have gone through in your life has meaning. And it's up to you to uncover the place where you are meant to go.

It doesn't matter if you have never been seen as magnificent by anyone before. It doesn't matter if no one in your life but you knows the truth of your experience. I know. You have a purpose. There are people in the world who need you to be healed. There are people who are depending on you to heal yourself so they can heal, too. Lots and lots of people are waiting for those of us who are "ill" to find our way out of the lost places and into the light.

I have been one of those who was considered very, very ill. No one understood what I was going through; they simply threw around the words of illness and deficiency. I was singing and talking to what I thought of as souls and angels—and what others called voices. I couldn't care for my children. I could barely eat or sleep. I believed that I was undertaking the healing of my soul and the souls of everyone in my life. I had two years of intense spiritual experiences that were called mental illness by everyone around me. No one ever said that I could be going through something magnificent. When I said I was a healer, they said I was grandiose and delusional. They said everything I was going through was meaningless, that all I could hope for was to be medicated and stay quiet about my experiences. I was initiated into the world of psychiatric hospitalization. More than once. I was locked up and held away from everything that I loved, and for many years afterward, I had to close down and disappear to live in the world at all. There are people who will always call what I went through mental illness. But I don't call it that anymore.

I have found a story that makes sense to me. I know that what I went through has beauty and magic and that I was doing the sacred work of healing my soul. It looked like it had no purpose to the people surrounding me in my life. All they wanted was for me to return quietly to the world they were comfortable with and to stop living outside of what was familiar to them. But I had to go to the places I went to. I had to go far from what was considered a normal life and into what seemed like utter chaos to be who I am today in the world.

Now I live a normal life. I take care of my children. I have a regular job. I drive a car and go to the grocery store on Saturdays. I do all the things that the people in my life wanted me to do back then, when I couldn't do as they asked; I couldn't simply stop what was happening to me. Now, my life is normal—yet it is also extraordinary. Now I know I was right when I told the doctors in the psychiatric hospital that I was a healer and that I was healing my soul and the souls of others. Everything that was supposed to happen from that place I was in is happening now.

It has taken over ten years and lots of hard walking to come to a place where I can tell you about it in a way that makes sense. But now it does make sense. And it becomes clearer and clearer all the time.

I want to show you how I uncovered the truth of who I am. I want to show you who you are. I am a healer. And you are, too. I was wounded. And if you are reading this, I bet you have been wounded, too. This world wounds healers who are like you and me. We are the healers that everyone sees as broken. We are the souls that get called mentally ill in a world that denies our truth and does not see any value in our experiences. Because the world is so dismissive of us, very few of us come out of the wounded place. But some of us do. And we can help the others. We don't have to stay wounded. We can find ourselves inside of the chaos. We can find ourselves even when everyone else is convinced that we are lost.

If more and more of us find ourselves, we can change the world. We can do what we are meant to do. We can be the healers we were born to be. You, too, can live a life that is about joy and not about illness. You can grow your roots and find your truest self.

But it requires something of you. It requires that you face your fear. Again and again. It requires that you listen to the voice inside your heart and believe in your own beauty. It requires you to make choices every day to do the biggest thing, the thing that has the most light. The thing your soul wants you to do.

Sometimes, doing the biggest thing requires you to appear small to others. Sometimes you have to listen to the outside voices just to get through the hard parts. Most important, you have to realize that being grounded is the first step and that you need to do all the things that are necessary in this world to sink your roots into the ground.

I came to this place by growing my roots. I grew my roots by putting my feet firmly on the ground. I had to walk slowly through all of the hard places first before I came to the place where there is more ease and light. I had to do the work of climbing the scraggly mountain before I could see the beautiful view. Now my feet are planted in a spot where I can recognize all of the loveliness that this life holds. The loveliness is mine, just as the hard places were—but even more so. You can find the loveliness, too. You can be who you are meant to be in this world if you take the steps you need to take to find your roots. You can be the one to hold your own experience. You can find your own story. You can own your life.

I have taken my life back. I know who I am. I have, step by step, released all of the ideas that others had about me and come into my own idea of myself, an idea that is based on who I have been my entire life. For a long time, I was an "ill" person to others and nothing more. But I was determined to discover who I am as a well person. I remembered that part of me that always sought beauty. I remembered the poet and the loving mother and the one who loves to sing who were always inside of me. That was hard. It was scary because one of the things that happens to you when you have been through what I have been through is that people tell you that who you are is very, very wrong. They tell you that you can't trust your own experience. You are called ill, and you are left to understand what that means about who you are. The part of you that is beautiful and whole gets bruised and broken because the people around you just don't know how to take you.

You can find yourself lost in a place where nothing seems to fit into what is ordinary. You find yourself in the world of dreams, yet you are awake. And the people in your life often don't react very well when you go to that place. You might do things that are outlandish and embarrassing. You might spend days lost in darkness or light. You might experience visions or have extraordinary experiences that can't be translated at the time into anything that seems to make sense. You might be, as I was, unable to be a normal person in the normal world.

When you have been knocked loose from the ordinary, you have to gather yourself back together and remember who you are all over again. You have to have time to find where your feet fit on the path again. Sometimes this takes years. For some, it can take a whole lifetime. The walking can be hard and uphill. But as long as you know you are going somewhere beautiful, you know it is worth it. And it is time for you to realize that you are going somewhere beautiful. You are going the place you have always been meaning to go. You are going to the place that only you can go. You are going to the place where your heart sings and where you light up the world around you.

When you know that you have a sacred destination, the hard walk, in itself, is not so bad. We are all meant to be healed. Our souls want every one of us to put all the pieces of ourselves back together again and be whole. That's why we are here. That's why we were chosen for this most sacred journey. Our souls know who we are. They know we are magnificent beings with so much to give to the world. All we have to do is decide to be our clearest selves, and we are supported every step along the way, especially when we begin to recognize that support. We have to walk where we are given to walk. The rest comes naturally.

The reason most of us don't realize that we have a such a special destination is that, when our soul was stretched out of our skin to take us there, we were treated as if we were merely lost and broken and not as if we were undergoing the most important journey of our lives. We were not honored as sacred beings. We were shut down, locked up, pushed away. At least I was. And that was harder to heal than anything else that I have experienced.

That is why I am writing this book. Because we need to see ourselves for the healers we are much sooner on the path. It is time for us to know the truth of who we are and to see the strength and beauty in the others like us. It is time for those of us who have become stuck in the life of illness and limitations to break free into the joy and wholeness that are meant to be ours. It is time for us to think of a new way to hold the people who go through what we have been through. It is time for us to be strong and clear and to heal what is ours to heal.

If you have been to the places I am describing, then accept this one truth: you are a healer. The people around you may see you as weak and broken. But inside, you have everything you need to walk to the place where you are whole. I am certain of you. I can see your magnificence. And I can see, from the flicker in your heart as you read these words that, you, too, are done with being broken. We can be done being broken together. I believe that all of us who leave the ordinary world and enter a place that makes no sense to those around us are healers. We can call it mania or psychosis, but I believe that those of us who go there are a part of a sacred undertaking that is meant to be a healing journey.

It is helpful to think of the experiences we are talking about as an actual place. When we go there, we know we are somewhere else—and so does everyone around us. Often, what makes sense to us when we are there makes no sense to others. Often, at the time, it also makes no sense to us. Sometimes it takes a while to come back, but when we do, we know that there is a place we have gone to that is beyond what we can explain.

We learn, often the hard way, that we have the tendency to go to a place where not everyone in the world goes. Those of us who go there are often the sensitive ones. We are the seekers and the ones who want to be healed. We are the ones who want to heal others. Some of us can spend our entire lives going in and out of that place.

For some of us it is a very dark place, a place where there are voices or visions that are full of torment, and it takes everything we have to stay in the world and remain good and kind when we are constantly being bombarded with darkness. I believe that the people who stand halfway in that dark place and halfway in the normal world are some of the bravest healers that our world has. They are the warriors fighting a sacred battle, yet their heroism is unseen by the rest of us. We call them broken, yet they are keeping the rest of us whole.

For some of us, that place is full of beauty and light. Sometimes we can feel very close to God. We can have voices and visions that tell us of great healing and love. The place I went to was mostly like that. I had experiences with the darkness, but I also had experiences of great bliss and understanding. I had many companions in that place who were kind and loving.

I came out of that place, and I can see it now from a different perspective. I can see how what I experienced there is now manifest in the world. It's not all literal. It's like a dream that needs interpretation. I can see now that I had to go there. I can see also that I had to experience that place in the exact way I did. Once you have gone to that place, you are never the same. It touches you, and you are changed. The trick is not to get stuck there. I have had the chance to heal from that place, as so many of us never do. But you can. I believe in you. All you have to do is take the first step of believing in yourself.

I am honored that you are here with me. Thank you for joining me in this journey. I can tell you about where I have been. And I can tell you how I have gone from being so very far away and ungrounded to being right here, right now. I can tell you about my roots. But it is up to you to find your own way of being grounded. It is up to you to sink your roots deep into the soil of who you are and who you were always meant to be. You will have support along the way, an unwavering support that comes from deep inside yourself, from the place that knows exactly who you are when you are whole. Our roots come from this very place. Our roots are the silent whispers of our soul that call to us, no matter how much chaos appears in our lives.

You can find your roots. You already know who you are. You just need to remove the dirt that has been piled up on the green shoots of your soul. It may be hard for you to believe in your own magnificence. It might sound impossible to know that you are a healer and that everything in your life has a purpose. You may feel very, very broken and lost, and the world might still be telling you that that is who you are. I have been there. There was a long time when all I could do was lie as still as possible and try to disappear. There was a long time when I could do nothing but what I had to do, and there was very little joy there. But the world had more for me to do than stay small. And so I began the journey. You can begin it, too. You can claim what is yours to hold close. You can uncover your most essential self.

Take my hand, and let's begin our walk together. The path is already cleared before us. Where we are going has already been determined. We are going to the only place our souls ever meant for us to go. We are going to the place where our light shines like the sun and the moon together. You and I each have our own map that relies solely on the stars. I already know we can get there. Soon you will know, too. We only have to start walking and trust our feet to guide us. Once we start walking, the rest will follow. We have a lot of beauty ahead of us still to be discovered. Let us begin.

A Space for Beauty and Grace—
Chapter 1—Finding Your Purpose Meditation

Sit quietly with your feet on the floor.

Close your eyes.

Take a deep breath in, and let it go.

Let go of all the cares of the day, feel them washing away as you focus on being right here, right now.

Notice how your body feels. Pay attention to whatever sensations come up. Don't try to change them. You are just in a place of noticing.

Take a moment to thank your body for carrying you to this moment.

Allow your thoughts to drift past. Don't attach or try to force anything to happen.

Just allow whatever comes to the surface to pass by like a cloud in the sky.

Now focus your attention inward.

Imagine yourself walking down a path that leads to a beautiful place.

You are heading away from the busyness of your usual environment and into a place of calm and the beauty of nature.

This can be a place you have been before or a new place.

It might be a forest or a mountaintop or the seashore.

As you walk, notice the sights around you.

What is the air like on your skin?

What are the smells like as you walk farther and farther down the path?

How do your legs feel as they carry you along?

You have now reached your destination.

You have come to your favorite place in nature.

Picture the scene before you.

You may be surrounded by tall trees or faced with a spectacular view of a valley, or perhaps you are standing at the edge of the ocean.

Let the beauty that surrounds you fill all of your senses.

As you stand in this place of beauty, ask yourself a question.

Ask the quiet place inside of you that knows everything what you need to know about your purpose.

Maybe an image will come, or a word or a phrase.

Who are you meant to be?

What magnificence lives in the quiet place inside of you?

What has your experience been leading you toward?

What is the one thing special thing that only you can do?

Ask yourself what you can take back to your life from this place that will help you remember who you really are.

Take that word or phrase or object, and tuck it away inside a safe place where you can find it whenever you need it.

Thank your inner wisdom for supporting you.

Take a last look at the beauty that surrounds you in this special place.

Know that it is always with you and that you can return to it at any time.

It is your powerful place.

Begin walking back down the path that led you here.

Walk slowly and comfortably, knowing that you are stronger than when you came.

Keep walking until you feel yourself back where you came from.

Take a deep breath, and slowly come back to the room.

Open your eyes as you feel ready.

CHAPTER TWO

Wholeness

It is a pretty strong statement to say that I am done being broken. It might seem grandiose to tell you that you can be done being broken, too. You might be wondering how I came to this place I am in now, where I don't feel broken anymore. You might want to know how I can say that I know that you are magnificent and that I believe in you and know that you are a healer who is meant to be healed. I can say these things because I have taken a journey that has led me, step by step, into the truth of my own soul and into the truth of yours. I will tell you the truth, that for a long time I believed the world when it told me I was broken. And because I believed that about myself, it was also the only thing I could believe about you. But I have come past that place on this path, sometimes called mental illness, a place that only allows for brokenness. Because I know who I am as a whole person again, it only makes sense that I also know that you are as brilliant and beautiful as you were in the moment you were born onto this earth. You are and have always been a shining light for the world. I hope that, as you read my words, you come to the place where you can see this for yourself. I hope you, too, find the place where you are whole.

First, I will tell you how I became lost. I started down the path that has led me here, to you, with a genuine desire to help people and embrace goodness. I was going through a divorce, and I had two small children, and I knew I needed to change my life. I knew I needed to have a calling aside from what I had been for the years of my marriage, a stay-at-home mom. I needed to be someone in the world that went beyond who I had been as a wife and a mother. What called to me was healing. Being well and healthy had always been a central theme in my life. I had always embraced a healthy lifestyle. Growing and learning had always been important to me. I was open to new things and new ideas. I was even more open after my husband and I split up; his disbelief in the unseen had kept me tied to the world in a way that I felt I no longer needed.

After my husband left me, I decided that I wanted to be a healer. I knew that I wanted to heal others. I had a deep commitment to helping others become whole. I began exploring everything I could about healing. I read lots and lots of books about people who were healers. I went to lots of workshops. I consulted healers of all types. I was open to everything that called itself a way of healing. After a year of all of this exploration and openness, I started having more and more experiences that took me out of the ordinary. For a while, those experiences could be explained by the books I was reading or the people I was seeking out who were considered to be healers of one kind or another. But then the experiences began to overtake me in bigger ways.

I became more and more ungrounded, and the things I was experiencing became stranger and stranger. Eventually, it got so far away from the ordinary that the people in my life stepped in, and I ended up in the hospital. To me, even then, it was a healing journey that I was on. I was sure that I was becoming a healer, that I was healing my soul and the souls of many others.

I had many experiences that were far from what I and others in my life had previously understood, yet I could do nothing but live through them. Some of those experiences were hard and traumatic, but mostly it was about healing and love and light. It was always about bringing others into the light. It was always about healing the souls of the other healers. Strangely enough, it was about being a writer and touching many people with my story.

During that time, what I was saying and doing was becoming increasingly strange and unbalanced to the people around me. I went very far away. It came to a point that there was no place left for me to go except to the hospital. There were no alternatives for my friends and family at that time. And so I learned the hard way how people are treated when they experience what I experienced. This experience could easily be called mental illness, but I also know now and knew then that it was the sacred calling of my soul. No one saw me as a healer. I became one of the broken ones.

I had all of the experiences that go with mental illness. I was spared from none of them: Being taken away in handcuffs more than once, in front of my friends and neighbors. Forced hospitalization in the state psychiatric hospital, twice in two years. Medication, despite my objection. Believe me, it is no fun when you are forced to lie on a metal hospital bed while two stern guards in rubber gloves stand over you, and the intimidating male nurse gives you an injection in your butt. And then you are a drooling zombie for days as the medication kicks in. I have never felt as much despair as when I was on those heavy, numbing anti-psychotic medications, which are used in situations like mine. They bring you back to earth, but they take away your light.

I spent two years in and out of the hospital and on and off anti-psychotic medication. I still tried to make sense of what I had experienced as a part of my journey as a healer. I still thought I was doing something special for the world. I still listened to the part of me that thought something about me was right. I didn't completely believe that I was broken, even though others tried to convince me that I was.

Until my last hospitalization, I hadn't fully realized that I was lost, even though I was not doing all the normal things people do anymore. I wasn't answering the phone, doing laundry, or going to the grocery store. I wasn't caring for my two small children. I knew they were safe with their father, and I knew inside that I just couldn't be with them the way they needed me to. I was spinning in the world of angels and souls. I was singing my way into the light. I was healing my soul so that, many years later, I could come to you and share these words with you. Of course, no one else saw it that way—which explains the magistrate and the police showing up at my door to take me away. Hence the locked wards and the people telling me I'd better straighten up or there would be consequences.

I remember the long days in the bleak state hospital during my last hospitalization; I had no idea when I would be home again, and I finally knew that I was lost. I got through the endless days and nights at the hospital by learning to become as small as possible. I found that, if I could lie completely still on the ugly, scratchy bed long enough, I could disappear to someplace else for just a little while.

It took four hospitalizations in two years for me to realize that I really had to start listening to the people around me and follow their rules if I had any hope of having a normal life again. When I went to the hospital, I didn't hide my belief that I was a healer on a sacred healing journey. I didn't cover up my experience that voices were talking to me and guiding me and loving me. I freely talked to the voices, which, I believed, belonged to souls; they were my friends and got me through the isolation of the hospital—even though they are also what kept me there. I didn't hide the fact that I was in a mysterious place inside of myself that the doctors, my friends, and my family didn't understand. For a while, leading up to the hospitalizations and while I was there, I said and did a lot of things that didn't make sense to the people around me. I know that the doctors and my family didn't want to hurt me; they only wanted to see me return to the person they were used to. But I also know now, after many years of listening to the people around me, people who told me that what I was experiencing meant nothing and that I was simply ill, that the place I went to was as real and necessary as any place I have been since or will ever go to again.

It took my last hospitalization, with its very real consequences, to knock me out of the place where I was actively engaging in my soul and back into the ordinary world. And coming back into that world, doing what other people expected of me, was a hard fall into a pit that took me years to climb out of. When I was at the hospital, my ex-husband applied for custody of my children. He said he was taking them out of state for a year and that I had to go to therapy and take medicine and be normal again before he would think of bringing them back. Being a healer didn't seem so important anymore. All that mattered was being a mother. Besides, no one believed that I was a healer, and the world I was in seemed determined to prove that I was not. I was now defined as a person who was lost. I was considered mentally ill. And mentally ill people need to listen to their doctors and stay quiet about their grandiose ideas. Mentally ill people need to stop living with their delusions.

I was discharged from the hospital for the last time, and my children were lost to me. I moved to my parents' home so I could be closer to them, though still five hours away, and my ex-husband agreed to bring them to see me every other weekend. It wasn't only my children whom I had lost. My former friends dropped out of my life without a word. They had had enough of me in my dramatic state. I had to leave my home, which I loved. I had no money and no job. I had nothing but a feeling of heaviness and a determination to never go to the hospital again and to get my children back. That would be my only light for many years.

In my search to become a healer, I had gotten very, very far away from the world around me. I had stretched out of my skin and into my soul. I had left the ordinary world completely behind me. People around me, in their desperation to save me, kept telling me that what I needed to do was get grounded. I needed to come back to where they were, where my children were. I hated that word, grounded, because I had gone to a place that was as far from the ground as a person could go. But, finally, when all was lost to me, including my children, I knew that they were right. I knew that the world I was in was a place where no one can stay. I knew I had to come back to what was familiar. I knew I had to listen to the people around me and become small again.

And that is exactly how I become grounded. I started out by becoming very, very small. I remembered, from my time in the hospital, how to disappear. So I disappeared. I lay quietly and waited for time to pass in between visits from my children. I did what I needed to do to stay in the world. I settled into the role of being someone who was ill. I let go of any ideas I had had about myself and healing. I had very little energy. Everything was a struggle. I felt utterly alone. I believed in nothing. I did everything I had to do to return to the world. I took my medicine without complaint. I saw my children when I was allowed to. I read to them and played endless games of hide-and-seek with them two weekends a month. I got some awful part-time jobs to earn a little money. I wasn't exactly a shining star in those jobs. People noticed that I was barely getting through. I watched a lot of television. I went to bed as soon as it was dark. I began getting very, very heavy. I gained a lot of weight.

But a year passed, and I stayed out of the hospital. I went to therapy, and my children came back to me, as my ex-husband had agreed. I was able to return to my home with them. I saw them regularly again. I was on disability, and I was very small inside myself, but when I got my children back, that is when I slowly, slowly started gaining myself and my life back. I kept doing the next thing and the next thing. It was very difficult, but I always did what I needed to do to go to the next step.

I got a job. Not a great job, but a quiet, low-stress job in a stationery store, a job that allowed me to go off disability. I worked at that job for several years. I did everything I needed to do to live my life. I continued to create a life for my children. I still felt lost. I didn't understand what had happened to me. I didn't understand why my journey to become a healer had shattered my life so completely. I felt very ashamed, and I felt as if everything that had happened to me had been because of a great mistake on my part. I believed that my mistake was to become too open. During that period of my life, after my divorce, I believed everything that purported to be about healing. I had no filter. I trusted too much. For a long time, I believed that I had caused myself to lose everything. I no longer wanted anything to do with healing. I just wanted to get through.

I can see now that everything in me had to shut down for me to be able to come back together again. When I was lost in the realm of my soul, I split wide open, and I lost my tether. I needed to go through a period of quiet and heaviness to re-root myself in the world. It even makes sense to me, now, that I had to be separate from my children. Losing them was the hardest thing that had ever happened to me—but it is what caused me to find the determination inside myself to do whatever I needed to do to get them back. I had learned everything about being held in the infinite world of souls and light, but I needed to learn once more about being grounded in the everyday world of the earth.

So, thankfully, life continued. My situation began to improve, and with each improvement, my happiness level grew. When I had been working for a while and doing well in the world again, I applied for legal joint custody of my children, and I got it. That was a big milestone for me. It proved to me that I was on the right path. I applied for and got a job in the mental health field. I was honest in my application about my own history of being a consumer of mental health services. That, along with my master's degree, got me in the door.

Getting a job working with people who were experiencing what I had experienced helped me in so many ways. In my world, I was the only one who had ever been to the hospital. I was the only one who had been taken away by the police for being too far from the world for people to understand. But suddenly, I was meeting many, many others like myself. Many of them were staff and soon became my friends. We all had our stories. And our stories were similar. Our stories were painful, but together we could laugh about them. I learned that many smart, beautiful people had been through what I had been through. Knowing that was my first step in overcoming my shame.

I couldn't continue to feel so bad about myself once I knew that I wasn't alone. I continued to heal from my experience. It got farther and farther away from me, and pieces started making sense. I lived for a while in a place of just being ordinary. For a while, that was just what I needed to be. But when people would ask if I was happy, I would say that I felt bogged down in the routine of life. And I continued being slow and heavy.

Then, one day, I had a realization that completely transformed my life from a life of getting through to a life of being whole and alive and being here with you now. One winter day, I was sitting on my sun porch after talking with an old boyfriend whom I had recently connected with on Facebook, and I realized that my whole life was focused on the worst thing that had ever happened to me. I realized that everything I said and did was based on the fear of it happening again. Going to the hospital and losing everything I loved, including my idea of who I was as a person, devastated me. It completely knocked me off my feet, and I was left gasping in the dirt. I had slowly climbed out of the dirt in the years since I had been out of the hospital, but I wasn't moving. I was standing still.

And that is when I started walking. Literally. I started my journey of healing, the journey that has led me here to you, by walking. I started off slowly. I walked thirty minutes a day, three days a week. But it was a beginning. Remember, I had learned to disappear in the hospital. And that was a habit that stayed with me for a long, long time. I still spent too much time lying still in my bed, and I didn't spend any time being active, other than going to work and caring for the everyday things we all take care of. So I started being active with walking. And I changed my diet. And I started facing my fear. I approached changing my life first with the physical and then with the mental. I decided not to just get through but to find myself.

It took a long time to get from the place I was in when I realized I needed to change to the place I am in now. I had a lot of walking to do to get to a place of wellness. My most essential self had been long hidden from myself. I had stopped writing, stopped singing, stopped lighting the candles and listening to music. I drank a little too much wine. I ate too many sweets, and I kept getting heavier and heavier. I don't think I was lost during that time, but I wasn't my most clear and beautiful self anymore, either. I was far from feeling beautiful.

Before I decided that I wanted to be a healer, before I started down the path that led to the hospital, I felt loved by my friends, and I felt like I knew who I was. I wasn't perfectly happy, but I felt alive and centered, and I loved living in the world. I created beauty, and I was a good mother. I had good friends; I danced and did yoga and sang. But the hospital and its effects on my life changed all of that. I no longer could do the things that I loved. Coming back to myself and my children took everything I had. I had no light for singing anymore. And besides, I felt like that part of myself, the innocent part that loved healing and beauty and feeling full of life, was the exact part of me that had taken me down such a painful path. I felt betrayed by my own soul.

So I covered her up and ignored her for a long time, until I could face her again. She scared me. I didn't want to risk knowing her. I wasn't sure where she would take me. But then one day, I knew it was time. I knew I needed to sing again. I knew I needed to write poetry and make lovely cups of tea and feel inspired and full of hope. And I knew that somehow, if I only trusted that I could once again return to the person that I had always been, long before I ever knew what it was like to be in the locked ward of the state psychiatric hospital, I could begin living again. Really living.

I call that part of me my most clear and beautiful self. And she is who is writing to you now. She is who I was before I was ever called mentally ill. And she is who I am now that I have my own understanding of my experience. Mine. Because I have learned to claim my story for myself. I have learned to call my experience my own. And because I have taken ownership of my own journey and my own soul, I can no longer be small. I can only be who I was always meant to be. And that is someone who is here to tell you that you can do the same for yourself. Your path won't look like mine. It will look like the path that only you can take. But it is yours. It will take work on your part to get to the place where you can call your life your own again. You will have to find your own way to walk there, and it might feel very hard at times. But I believe that you can do it. And I know you can find the strength inside of you that you need to take the journey to wholeness. You have a most clear and beautiful self. Don't let anyone or any experience take that truth away from you. If that self is buried, you have what you need to find her under the dirt—just as I had what I needed to find my own. I know it is a strong statement, but it is the absolute truth. I am done with being broken. And I hope that if you're ready, we can be done being broken together.

A Space for Beauty and Grace— Chapter 2—The Quiet Place Meditation

Sit quietly with your feet on the floor.

Close your eyes.

Take a deep breath in, and let it go.

Let go of all the cares of the day; feel them washing away as you focus on being right here, right now.

Notice how your body feels. Notice your breath gently going in and out.

Notice the pulse inside of you that is full of the feeling of aliveness.

Notice the hum of energy that is always with you in the quiet place.

Now start paying attention to the quiet place.

Let any thoughts go, and just focus on the silence that lives inside of you.

It might take you a little while to recognize it if you haven't been paying attention to it.

But it is there.

Focus your attention on your heart.

Bring your hands up, and place them gently over your heart.

This is where your quiet place lives in your body.

Take a few moments just to notice the quiet inside of you, in your heart.

Now ask the quiet place if it has a message for you.

Listen, and know that your quiet place is responding, even if you can't hear anything now.

Tell your quiet place that you want it to be your friend.

Tell it that you would like to hear its wisdom in your life.

Now thank your quiet place for always supporting you.

Tuck away anything that it has offered you today, and know that you can always return to it and trust in its presence.

Take a deep breath in, and slowly come back to the room.

Open your eyes when you are ready.

CHAPTER THREE

Walking

The path to wholeness always begins with you. It is your path, and the map is inside of you. Just as it is helpful to think of where you went when you left the ordinary as a place, it is helpful to think of where you will be when you are whole and well as a place. When you know you have a destination, you can do what you need to do to get there. I picked my destination after I had come out of the place where I was lost but hadn't yet walked to the place where I was found. I knew my destination was me. And I knew that to find myself, I had to walk to the place where I was whole. I didn't know exactly what I would meet along the way or where exactly I would find myself. But I knew I had a place to go that was mine. And so I started walking.

It really can begin with something as simple as that. Walking. If you're heavy and slow and bogged down by all the ways you have been broken, start with a walk. That is what worked for me. Taking a literal walk is what started me down the path to where I needed to go. Exercise heals your body and your mind from the inside out. Your heart, your lungs, and your brain change when you exercise. And so does your spirit. Walking gave me more energy. It transformed me from someone who was afraid of physical activity to someone who loved to get my heart beating and my blood pumping. It changed what I believed about myself. Through walking, I discovered my roots.

I also started paying attention to what I ate. I made good choices of fruits and vegetables and foods that fueled my body and gave me lots of good nutrients. I ate what made my body feel alive and healthy, and I let go of habits that kept me heavy. I began to go to a yoga class. I started paying attention to my breath.

I made a commitment to keep a journal where I wrote down the things I did for myself every day. I wrote down everything I ate and where and how far I walked and how long I practiced yoga. I did that for over three years, and it was very grounding. I made a commitment to myself that I would emerge from the heaviness that had been weighing me down and keeping me afraid and broken for all the years since I had been in the hospital. My diet/exercise journal was a big part of my healing. It kept me aware of the good choices I needed to make every day.

More than anything else, wholeness is about choices. Our choices are what lead us down our own special path to wellness. Every day, many times a day, I remembered my bigger goal of finding my way back to my true self. When I faced the endless pieces of cake or brownies that show up in our environment without our control, or I had the choice of sitting on the couch and doing nothing or going for a walk instead, I always remembered my goal.

I walked and I did yoga and I ate really well. Those were my three ways to begin to find myself again. Those were the steps I took to be grounded. I was looking for the sacred spark of my soul that had been lost, but in order to find it, I had to start with my body. To come back to myself fully, I had to start with the physical. Walking outside got me connected to nature again after a long time of sitting inside and being still. I began to notice the sky and the trees. This eventually returned me to my spirit.

I loved the feeling of the sun and the fresh air on my skin. In the very beginning, it was hard because I was so heavy. But it got easier and easier, and I began to love it. I started off only walking on the flat routes in my neighborhood. I started off walking for just short periods of time, a few days a week. I always recorded it in my journal. As time passed, I could feel myself changing. My mind was calmer. My lungs felt alive and energized. My heart felt clean and clear. I went to a yoga class once a week at the library. It helped me be in my body in a strong and flexible way. It also calmed my mind.

After about a year of walking and going to yoga class, I reached a new level of wellness. I began walking for an hour almost every single day. I started walking not just in the flat places; I started tackling the big hills in my neighborhood. I started doing yoga at home every day for forty minutes. What had at first been a struggle, after a year became a joy. Taking care of my body led to me to more and more wellness, and for the first time in a long time, I also began to be able to take care of my soul.

I started writing again. Writing in my journal had always been a big part of my life. I had a notebook full of poetry, and writing was a path of self-discovery for me. It was a way for me to process my thoughts and feelings. It was a way for me to record my life. It was like a friend that I could talk to whenever I wanted. It was a saving grace. Returning to writing was a big step in returning to myself. For many years after the hospital, I didn't write because I was too busy staying still. Writing opened me back to my heart.

Walking inspired me to start singing again. I felt so much joy being outside and moving my body that I just had to sing. I have always loved learning my favorite songs and singing them to myself or to my children, when they were small. My biggest dream for myself is to have my home be filled with music. I want to learn to sing with the guitar. I also started listening to my long-quiet collection of CDs. I listened to music while I did yoga, and I began listening to it while I was cleaning or at night before I went to bed. I even got the candles out and started lighting them at night while the music played. This might sound like nothing special, but when I was still being quiet, I had given up music and candlelight. I had given up everything I loved in the process of returning to normal after I had gone so far away.

The hardest part of returning to myself was facing my fear. I started with the physical, but I couldn't ignore who I was mentally and spiritually. And who I was mentally and spiritually was a person who was lost in fear. I didn't trust myself. I knew that my most clear and beautiful self was inside of me. And I knew that I had to uncover her and be with her again. But there had been so much pain and loss. I had been devastated. I had gone to places I never knew I could go to. I had lost everything that I held dear. My life had become about what was wrong with me, when for so long before it had always been about what was right. Before I went to the hospital, I had loving friends, and I knew who I was. I believed in goodness, and I believed in healing. I believed that if I was good and kind, then good and kind things would happen in my life. I was innocently seeking my true path, and I was unaware that such trauma could happen to me while I was doing only what I knew to do: exploring the calling of my soul to be a healer.

I did face my fear. Even though it was hard. I still face it, whenever it comes up. It comes up less and less now that I have faced the biggest parts of it. When I see it now, I recognize it for what it is, and it loses its power. It is just an arrow pointing to the next place and not something that can stop me from living anymore. When you face your fear, something inside of you rises up to help you, and it always takes you to the next place. To come to the place of wholeness, I went for long daily walks in my neighborhood, but I also had to walk every day in the places inside myself that were still heavy and broken. When I began looking for my most clear and beautiful self, it had been many years since I was lost in the world of the unseen, but inside, I was still lost to myself. Facing my fear was my path to being found. I kept having to be brave, over and over.

The thing I was most afraid of was my own spirit. I had put aside any idea I had of God or my soul. I had been numb and quiet for so long, and I wanted to be alive again, but to do that, I needed to face my spiritual self. But I needed to do it in a way that felt very safe and grounded. So I began with nature. I wanted to pray, but it frightened me to try to connect with anything bigger than myself. I found a way to pray that kept me grounded. I prayed under my favorite tree in the park while I was out walking. My prayers started out simple. I asked God to help me be strong and clear and beautiful. I asked the tree to hold my prayers, and I touched its trunk and looked up through its branches to the sky.

I did this every time I walked. Sometimes I would vary the prayer, depending on what was going on in my life. But at first, I kept it as simple as possible. Once I began to pray again, I really opened up my heart to who I truly am. I am a person who has always longed for a deep connection with God. By praying, I began to feel connected to myself again at my center. And then I started to meditate. That was even scarier than praying. But I faced my fear and started slowly. Meditation was something that I couldn't do during the years when I was coming back to myself after my soul broke free. I wasn't grounded enough to go to the places meditation takes you. I couldn't even pick up and read books about healing or spirituality during that time. If I did, I felt instantly terrified and had a spinning, ungrounded feeling.

I started off with meditation, after I had become grounded in my body through exercise, by just paying attention to my breath and the sensations in my body. Over time, I developed a way to meditate that works very well for me. I focus on my connection to the physical world, and through that, I am able to connect with the spiritual. I began by picturing my tree in the park in my mind when I meditated. I would focus on its roots and imagine my own roots going deep into the earth. I began to expand to the other trees nearby, and I pictured all of the trees around me listening and communicating with each other through their roots. I began to picture my tree as a tall column around me in which I was safe and completely connected to earth and sky and to all the other trees.

I also began meditating on my connection to the earth through the foods that I ate. I would picture each thing that I had eaten that day and where on the earth it had come from. I would picture the reservoir that brought me the water for my tea and the tea plantation the brought me the tea leaves. I would picture the cow that gave me my yogurt and the oats that made my granola. I would imagine the actual plant or the actual tree that each particular food grew from. This was a practice of gratitude, and it was also a way to connect to my body and the world around me. It was an inspiration to eat foods that were as close to their natural state as possible.

I began to think about and ask for the things that made my heart sing. During yoga I developed a practice of saying yes to all of the things I wanted in my life. I said yes to mothering and writing and music and beauty and friendships new and old. I started saying yes to having new experiences in my life that brought forth all the things I loved. I started saying yes to who I wanted to be in the world.

The other thing that frightened me and that I had to face in order to find myself is what I call being big. When we are afraid of something, we have a choice. We can stay with the fear, or we can do the thing that requires us to move beyond the fear into our biggest self. I am not talking about fear that keeps us from doing things that would make us unsafe. I am talking about the fear that shows up every time we are faced with a choice that will lead us to the next place where we need to go to be whole. Those choices show up all of the time. We are constantly being given opportunities to grow. The only thing between us and our most clear and beautiful selves is the layers of our fear.

I faced my fear at each layer, and each time it got easier. I learned to recognize my fear for what it was, and I learned that I could look at my choices and choose the one that would lead me to the place I wanted to go. At first, when I started walking, I was afraid of going over a bridge that leads to the downtown part of my city. I had lots of reasons: there was too much traffic, it felt too exposed, I just didn't like it, etc. But I wanted to be able to walk on the downtown mall and the neighborhoods around it. I realized it was just a fear, and sometimes the only way to get past a discomfort is to push through it. So I started walking there in spite of my reluctance to cross the bridge. After I walked there a few times, the discomfort completely went away. Once I got over my fear of the bridge, I began walking downtown all of the time. It was awesome, and I spent many beautiful days there sitting on the mall writing and drinking tea. That is what I mean about being big. You do the thing you are given to do, and you push through the discomfort that tries to keep you small.

These same kinds of choices show up in everything we do. When we are having a conversation with someone we love, we can choose to say the thing that comes most from our heart or we can avoid it and stay small. If our biggest dream is to sing but instead we stay quiet, we can face our fear and start by singing in the bathtub. If we love flowers and always long for them but think we have to have a boyfriend to give them to us we can begin by buying ourselves a beautiful bouquet and putting it in our favorite vase in our bedroom. No matter where we have been, we can start our path to wholeness by following the light inside of us.

You may be like I was: so broken by the world that your light is covered by layers and layers of dark, mucky fear. But you have a light. Maybe you are a poet. Or you love boxing. Do the thing that calls you over and over again. Take all day to read the paper at the dining room table on Sunday, and drink lots of black coffee in a beautiful mug, and eat your favorite pastry. Take the first step to do the thing you have wanted to do your whole life. Do what is yours to do to honor who you are inside your most true self. Start small, and remember your destination. You are on your way to living your most clear and beautiful life.

As you can see, everything I did to make myself well comes back to a central theme: being grounded. If you are like me—someone who goes to the places that are far away from the ordinary—you have to find your roots in order to be whole. I found my roots by taking care of my body first. After I had been really taking care of my body for a while, I was able to start taking care of my soul. I began to live again from my heart. My heart was right there, waiting for me to notice it. It always told me the next thing to do. That is how I have come to you today. I am sitting in my cozy home at my beautiful writing desk, and

I am telling you how I went from being so very lost to where I am now, to where I know who I am again. I got here exactly as I described: one step at a time.

Someone recently asked me if I was afraid of going back to where I was when I was in the hospital. And the answer now is no. Because I know how I have gotten here. I know that I did the work; I did the walking. I went through it all, layer by layer. I couldn't have said that I wasn't afraid when I began walking. I was still afraid for a very long time. But I faced it. It took a lot of effort to get here. And that is why I know that it is mine. I have my own truth now. I have my own path. I used to believe that everything that happened to me was some horrible accident caused by everything I did wrong. I used to be victim of my experience. I could not understand how my life had turned out the way it did.

But now I can see it for what it is to me. It began with my quest to become a healer. And to become a true healer, I needed to first heal myself. I needed to go through all the places that the healers like you and I go to. I needed to be lost for a while in the places of the soul where only some of us are chosen to go. And then, for many years, I needed to be slow and heavy and still, until I was able to fully come back from those places. I needed to be fully planted in this world again before I could even begin to understand my purpose or my truth. And when I was done with coming back to earth, I needed to find my spirit again. So I started walking toward my own light. As you have seen, it was a long walk with a lot of clearing the path along the way. There were the brambles and fallen trees of my fear. But I made my way through. And so can you.

The most important thing I have realized about deciding to find my way back into the world again once I had been lost from it is that I was supported. This is also true for you. The place in you that loves what you love is waiting for you to find her. She wants you to be whole. She wants you to wake up in the morning and feel alive and free. She wants you to find your purpose and live inside of it every day. She wants you to live your most clear and beautiful life. There is nothing so broken about you that you can't ever be whole. You may have been lost to the world, but you have the path inside of you to be found again. Remember, you are magnificent. You have something to do that is yours, and if you begin it you will have the support you need to find out what that is. Your heart already knows. Make a commitment to yourself that, no matter what it takes, you are going to uncover your brilliance. Decide today that you are going to walk to the place on the mountain where you can see the beautiful view of your own possibilities. You can begin it. It is yours.

A Space for Beauty and Grace—
Chapter 3—Nourishment Meditation

Sit quietly with your feet on the floor.

Take a deep breath in.

Gently notice the pattern of your breath.

Notice the rise and fall of your belly.

Now go back over in your mind what you have nourished your body with today.

Think about the first thing that you drank.

Imagine where that thing that you drank came from before it came to you.

If it was water, picture the reservoir in your town where it comes from. Or picture it flowing beneath the earth where it comes into your well.

Picture how the water that you drank today is connected to all of the other water on the earth. Picture the rivers and streams and the seas and rain clouds that bathe the earth and give you the water that you need.

Now think about the food that you have eaten. Think about each of the ingredients of the food that you put into your body. If you had a peanut-butter sandwich, think of the peanuts growing beneath the earth, the salt coming from the sea, and the wheat growing in the fields that the bread was made from.

Do this with everything you have eaten today. If you like, you can also picture all the hands that brought this food to you.

Now take a moment to give thanks for the nourishment that you received today, the nourishment that keeps you healthy and whole and alive.

Honor your body and the body of the earth for bringing you to this moment.

Take a deep breath in.

When you are ready, open your eyes and return to the room.

CHAPTER FOUR

Healer

Once you have been labeled as mentally ill, it can be difficult to believe that you are a healer and that who you are and what you have been through has a purpose. But I found that everything about the experiences that led me to the hospital was about healing. I got to the place I was in by exploring everything that I could about being a healer and healing my soul. I actively told people that I was a healer at the time, and in the beginning, I truly believed that my experiences had meaning and that I was doing the work of my soul that I had been specially chosen to do. The experiences I had with that other place were all-consuming and brilliant and sometimes very, very hard. But I believed that the only thing I could do was flow with them and that I was on a sacred journey that would lead to the healing of myself and many others. I only gave up on the idea that I was a healer after I lost everything and everyone around told me to be quiet and stop thinking about it and just try to be as normal as possible.

So I did my best to become ordinary. The medication was a help. It took me out of the high places and brought me back to a place where I could function in the ordinary world. Over time, it also made me very, very heavy. But I think now that that was a necessary state for me, after I had become so very light. With effort, on the outside I started to look ordinary, if not actually very happy. But I had to hide a lot of what I was still experiencing so that I could appear normal. I did the things I needed to do in the world, and I accepted that I was far from being a healer. I accepted what people around me told me. Everyone said that the place I had gone to was a place people go to who are ill and that it was meaningless in the world that I had to live in and the best thing I could do was leave it alone.

And, if I wanted to get my life back and be okay in the world again with the people surrounding me, I had to do just that. I had to leave thoughts of healing and light and angels and souls alone. I was still touched by those things. My experiences with that world changed me forever. I couldn't even begin to understand what any of it meant. I just had to heal from the fact that I had been there, and I had to do my best to return to what other people were familiar with and focus on living day by day.

I have already described to you how I came out of that period of being heavy and shut down to being in a place where I could live again from my heart. But I want to tell you how I came to believe in my own self as a healer again. And most important, I want to share with you how I have come to the understanding that you are a healer, too.

Everything I learned about that place that I went to, which can't be explained by the ordinary, I had to learn slowly, over time, after I had been out of it for a long while. If I wanted to have my life back, I had to do everything I needed to do to stay out of that world. I had to choose to stay far from that place where I now could so easily go. It is a place that has a strong call once you have been there, but in order to heal my life, I couldn't keep going there. I had to stay away from all of the things that could still take me there and just immerse myself in the world that is normal.

So, for many years, that place was as lost to me as I was to myself. I had constant reminders that I had been there. I relived many of the experiences I had there in my mind over and over. When I first got out of the hospital, it was hardest to stay out of that world. But I knew I couldn't go there anymore. I knew that my children and my family needed me to be in this world.

When I made the commitment to stay as much in the ordinary as possible, I began to heal. It took a long time—many years. And for a long time, most of what I had experienced while I was in that other place didn't make much sense. It was too big to think about, really. It was the world of dreams that I had been to while I was awake.

That place can cause us to do all kinds of things that aren't safe or make no sense. I ran out into traffic to get away from my friend who was trying to help me. I held that same friend down to the ground because I thought evil was after her. I saw two suns in the sky. These are the types of things that can happen when we are there. That place is not a place where we can stay and also be able to live in this world. People step in and try to help us when we go there, and usually, they are right—we need them. When we go to that place, we need others around us to keep us safe because we are so far away that we can't take care of ourselves.

I am not denying that when we are in that place, we make little sense to the people around us and we are lost to the ordinary world. But what I have learned over the years since I have come back from that place completely is that that place is sacred. It is the place of our soul. It is the place of visions and dreams. It is the place of healing and purpose and light. It can also be the place where we hold the darkness of the world. It is the place of magical journeys and brave heroes. It is a place that only certain people go to. And I believe that those of us who go there have a purpose for entering that world of the soul. And that purpose is about healing.

When we go to that place, we are on a healing journey. We go there to see the hugeness of our own being. We go there to be enfolded in the mystery. We go there to bring something back to the everyday world from the world of the soul. While we are there, we need to be loved and supported. While we are there, we can't do all of the things we are asked to do in this world. We have stretched out of our skin and are in the place of unseen.

I believe that place we go to is the place of healing. When we come back from there, we have the opportunity to reach levels of healing for ourselves and others in our lives that not everyone has access to. Because we have broken through to the soul place, we can be even more whole and free than most people ever have the chance to be.

But we have to do what we need to in order to come fully back from that place. And we have to do everything we can to keep ourselves from living there. We have to decide that we are going to fully live in this world in order to heal and fulfill our sacred purpose.

I can't say exactly when the things that happened to me when I was in that place started making sense in this world. But over time, they have. At first, it doesn't make sense in the way that reading a book about science makes sense. It makes sense in the way that reading a book about fantasy makes sense. You have to be open to interpretation and to using the imaginative parts of your mind. Many of the visions and experiences that I had when I was in that other place do make literal sense now. I am doing what I was called to do then. I am sharing my vision of healing and light with others. I didn't know it would be so hard to get here where I can feel myself healed. I didn't know I would have to lose everything I loved in order to find it again.

I didn't know that being a healer meant I first had to heal myself. I didn't know that I had to go to the soul place so that I could return and show others like you who go there, too, how to come back.

I always knew the place I went to was sacred. Only when everyone in my world told me that it was not was I able to give up what I always knew and believed about my sacred purpose and accept their view—that I was simply and terribly ill. That was my path to wholeness. I had to be one of the lost ones. I had to be locked away and shut down. Then I had to do everything I needed to do inside myself so I could be found. I had to rediscover the sacred healing nature of my soul one step at a time. I had to let go of what others believed about me and return to what I believed about myself. I had to find my own version of my story, a version that makes sense to me.

You can find your own version of your own story. I am no different from you. I have been to all the same places you have. I have seen the worlds of darkness and of light. I have ridden high above the clouds and have come crashing down into the lowest part of the earth. I have been everywhere there is to go in the place of the soul. And I have had to work hard at coming back to the place where it all makes sense again.

It can someday make sense. What is important is not the exact thing that you experienced when you were in the high place. It is not your job to focus on that world and make sense of it if it still seems impossible to understand. The understanding from that place comes slowly, over time, when it is ready. Your job is to come back here. Your job is to be where the people who love you can see you clearly.

I am not telling you that you are a healer so you can stay lost. I am telling you that you are a healer so that you can find yourself. Your soul is sacred. You are a hero on a magical journey. You have a light that can light up the world. You have a purpose that only you can fulfill. It is time for you to find it.

It's true that the people around you might see you as lost and broken. And maybe it's even true that you still are. But there is more for you. No one needs to stay broken. We can all do what we need to do to be whole.

My path to wholeness was a long one. But I claimed it as my own. When we get defined in the world as mentally ill, one thing that often happens to us is that we forget that we are strong. The people around us are convinced of our weakness, and we become convinced of it too. It took me a long time and many layers to discover my strength, but then I realized it had been there all along.

I am strong not just because of what I have been through but because of who I am. One of the most important things I did for myself so that I could heal was to remember who I was before I went to the hospital. I had to remember who I had always been. I had to rediscover my heart after having been lost to myself.

That is my strength, and it is also yours. Who are you on the inside? Who have you always been in your heart? What does the magic inside of you whisper in your ear when you stop to listen? You didn't say when you were a child that you would like to go to the psych ward. You never planned on becoming someone the world sees as mentally ill.

But you were given this life that you hold now in your hands. Maybe you have been letting other people hold it for you because you don't remember who you are since you have gone to the broken places. Maybe other people have been in charge of where you go and what happens in your life because you haven't known how to hold it for yourself.

You can reach out your hands and take it back. It is yours. It's your life, your heart, your journey, your purpose. You have just as much right to own your own story as anyone else in this world. You can find the path that leads you out of the lost places and into the brilliance of who you are meant to be.

All of us are given something that we have to overcome in this world. Those of us who are called mentally ill because of where our souls take us to are no different from the rest of the people who live beside us. It's only the world that sets us apart. People think we have some special weakness that makes us less valued than the people who never go where we have gone. Our lives become about what is wrong with us, and everyone forgets what is right.

The opposite of that is true. Those of us who go to the places outside of the ordinary, the place called mental illness, have instead a special kind of strength. We are chosen to walk a sacred path. We are chosen to see what remains unseen to most. We are chosen to heal ourselves all the way to our souls.

In order to heal your soul you first have to see it. You have to recognize it for what it is. I went deep into the world of my soul, and I came back. I couldn't be here now with you if I hadn't gone there. And I also couldn't be here if I never decided that I needed to come all the way back.

When we return fully from the world of the soul, we can act as gatekeepers. We can help others who need healing get where they need to go. I am certain that there are people in your life who need you. One person can't heal without many others around him or her healing as well. We are all a part of the same circle. We are all connected, and we are all walking to the place where we are meant to go, to the place where we are whole.

Remember the word of your soul. Magnificence. That is who you are, really. Your possibilities go beyond even what I can see for you. I know that you are a healer because I know that we are all meant to be healed. I know that you have a purpose because I know that you were born into this world to share your light with others. I know this about you, and I want you to know this about yourself. It is time for you to claim your story. It is time for you to find your roots.

It is time for you to become who only you can be and do what only you can do. If you have been lost, it is time for you to be found. Stop and listen to the voice inside of you that knows everything. What does it say? What is the next step, the one thing that is yours to do now to begin it? Listen to that voice. At first it might come in a whisper. But it is there. Find that little spark that lives inside of you, and begin your journey into your own heart.

If you have heard lots of voices that led you far away, it might be hard at first to recognize the voice that is most true. But there is something inside of you that knows the difference. There is a wisdom and strength inside of you that no one and nothing can touch. It is yours.

Take a breath and find your courage and go into the quiet place inside of you. In that place, you are always supported. In that place, you are always whole. You have always been meant to go to the place where you are whole, even when you appeared lost. You went to that exact place of brokenness in order to be where you are now, in a place where you can understand who you are and what you are meant to do.

It is time to embrace yourself for who you really are. It is time to honor the places you went to and the person you have become as sacred. You are a healer. You are a light for others. You are a blessing to the world. I honor you. Now you can begin to honor yourself.

A Space for Beauty and Grace—
Chapter 4—Caring for Your Feet

Do you lie awake in bed at night with your head spinning and your thoughts racing? Get out of bed. And pay attention to your feet. Take some sweet-smelling massage oil. Lavender is a good choice. Now gently massage your feet. If you have been really racing in your head, it is good to massage your whole legs and work your way down to your feet. When you go back to bed after paying attention to your feet, your body will feel different. You will feel warm and heavy and relaxed, and the energy will have moved from your head down into your lower body.

My friend's daughter was having racing thoughts and bad dreams. My friend started massaging her feet at night before bed, and the bad dreams completely went away. My friend and her daughter had created a lovely new bedtime ritual that neither one of them wants to ever give up! Our bodies can help us and be our allies instead of our enemies. Sometimes we just need to do simple things, like paying attention to our feet, to support our bodies.

CHAPTER FIVE

Support

To live your most clear and beautiful life, you have to have support. When you go to the places we have gone to, where no one around us understands what we are saying or doing and they just want us to stop going there, we can begin to feel very, very alone. In fact, our behavior may drive people away from us. That certainly happened to me. I had lots of close friends before I broke my soul open. Afterward, I had very few.

The place to start with support is inside yourself. You have to decide that you are not going to be lost to yourself anymore. You have to decide to uncover your inner strength. You can begin by remembering who you really are. I know that you have been wounded and hurt. I know that you have gone far away from where you ever expected to go. I also know that it's likely that, since you went to those places, you also have experienced the trauma of what happened to you when you went there. You know what it is like to be locked in, to be pushed aside, to be told that you are nothing. Maybe people have been telling you what you have to do for so long that you have forgotten how to do anything for yourself.

Even so, I invite you to remember. Just as the path to wholeness in your body and your mind can begin with something as simple as taking a walk, the path to finding your inner strength can begin with something as simple as a moment of silence. Take a deep breath, and go inside. All the strength and all the answers you will ever need are in the quiet place inside of you.

It may be hard at first to find your quiet place. You may even have dark voices that pick at you and try to steal your peace. It might be scary to go inside yourself. I know that, at first, it was for me. I had so many experiences where my mind and my soul took me to places that I just didn't want to go anymore. I was afraid that, if I got quiet, I would go right back to those places.

But the quiet inside of us is a gift that we all are born with. If you decide to find it, nothing will keep it from you. It is yours. Your strength is your own. You wouldn't be here reading this if you were weak or hopeless or lost. You have so much more inside of yourself than you have ever acknowledged before. Once you start to acknowledge the truth, the truth becomes bigger. The truth is that you can uncover your magnificence just by deciding that you will.

To begin, sit in a comfortable chair and turn off the distractions of music or television. Start with just your breath. Pay attention to your breath, and just let in the quiet that surrounds you. Once you have found the quiet around you, you can focus on the quiet inside of you. The quiet inside of you might come with a feeling or a picture or a word. Keep returning to the quiet that you have found again and again. Ask the quiet place for support.

After I found my quiet place, I discovered that I could ask it questions, and I would always get an answer. Sometimes the answer would come directly in words, and sometimes I would just sit quietly and nothing appeared to be happening but afterward, I would simply know the next thing I needed to do. Finding the support that is inside of you is important to take you where you need to go to be whole. With the support of the quiet place, you can do what it is that is yours to do. Without it, you can keep wandering around endlessly in the lost places or in the places where you are not exactly lost, but you are not moving toward wholeness; you are just standing still.

After you have found the support that is alive inside of you, it is time to find the support that is everywhere around you in the world. When we think of our support systems, we think of people. And people are important. But they might not come first if you have been without them for a while.

I started with the trees. I told you how I connected my spirituality to the tree in my neighborhood by sending my prayers up through its branches every day when I walked. But it was much more than that. I gathered my strength from something as simple as the trees, something that I could touch and see in the world everywhere I went. I pictured their roots and my own. I pictured tree after tree spreading out all over the earth, each connected to others by its roots under the ground. I started with the actual trees in my neighborhood and spread out to all the trees everywhere. And I asked them to support me just as they support the earth.

There is so much beauty and strength in the world around us. It is kind of ridiculous for us to believe that we are all alone when we are supported by everything that grows and lives and stands beside us. We can be connected to everything; all we have to do is consciously choose to be.

My touchstone is the tree, but I also find support from other aspects of nature.

Sometimes when I meditate, I concentrate on all of the elements. I envision the water that flows all over the earth and in my body. I picture waterfalls and rivers and streams and the ocean, all flowing together to bathe the earth. I picture the water cleansing me and washing away any pain or fearful places. I give thanks for the water that keeps me alive in my body and in the world.

I also focus on the fire that lives in the center of the earth and warms and heals my body. And the rocks and mountains that are silent and solid and hold the healing and strength of the earth. You could focus on the animals that mean the most to you. You can find a special thing in nature that calls to you like the tree calls to me. It doesn't matter what you call upon; what matters is that you let go of the idea that you are all alone in the world battling your life by yourself—and realize that you are as much a part of everything around you as everything else on the planet is. You can draw support from the world around you, and you can know that the world will always give it to you. You no longer have to be lost in your mind. You can be found in your body, which is a part of this bountiful earth.

Once you are strong from the support of everything around you in the natural world, you can begin to find the support that is everywhere from the people who live here. If you don't have a lot of people in your life right now whom you feel supported by, you can still feel a connection to others. One of the layers of fear that I had to unravel in order to be whole was about being alone and also about being a victim.

I felt that everything in my life was up to me to handle. I felt as if I was always by myself and had no one to depend on for anything. And when I looked into my fear, I also discovered that I didn't just think I was alone, I also thought that other people were actively trying to hurt me. I had so much pain from when I went to the hospital and I felt like people there forced me to comply with them without honoring who I was. But that was just the trauma that I carried with me—and I could heal that. What was harder to realize was that I also carried a deeply held fear that whenever I put myself out in the world, the people around me would try to hurt me. I was terrified of being who I was meant to be in the world, not because of what I would become but because of how I thought people would treat me.

I spent my time believing that whatever I did that was good would be attacked or dismissed by the people around me. I didn't believe that I was supported. I believed that I was fighting a constant battle against people's smallness. I also felt that, if I really did become my most clear and beautiful self, people would respond with spite and jealously and meanness and not support me. Or that they simply wouldn't understand what I was trying to say and do. I kept thinking that people wouldn't understand me.

So I decided to change my belief from the inside out. Instead of thinking that people would try to hurt me for being beautiful and doing the work of my soul, I began to picture all of the people in my life supporting me. My coworkers, my ex-husband, my family, my friends. I began to see them as loving and kind toward me. I imagined that people would delight in me and love me and that they wanted me to succeed. And I pictured you, who I knew would read my words, supporting me in being myself and speaking my truth so that I could be who I needed to be in the world.

I began to focus on the goodness and light that exists in the world instead of on the fear of the imagined darkness. I began to honor the fact that there are people who love me and understand me, and I began to let go of the thoughts or worries about the people who don't. Really, the people who don't understand us or would judge us or intentionally cause us harm aren't our people.

They don't belong to us. We don't need them. We need the people in our lives who always want the best for us and whose only wish is to love us. Those are the people we need to go to for support. And if we don't see them quite yet in our lives, we can hold the space for them in our hearts until they are ready to come.

When we start looking at the people around us as loving and supportive of us, something magical happens. It begins to be true. Those people start showing up in our lives. I have often told my story to groups of people, and there is often a question that comes up. People wonder if I am afraid that people will judge me or if I am afraid that I could lose my job or something else I value in my life because people who don't understand would try to harm me. People have approached me, people who want to be able to share their story openly, but they are afraid they would be too exposed and vulnerable.

The truth is that once you begin to honor yourself and your path as sacred, none of that matters anymore. The more you see yourself as supported, the more supported you will be. The negative voices lose their power when you are living your truth in the world. If you are no longer ashamed and fearful and you focus on what is right instead of what is wrong, you will find support at every step of the path.

I haven't talked yet about the support of the divine or of God. When you are connecting to the support that is inside of you and in everything and everyone around you, you are connecting to the divine as well. Spirituality can be hard for people who go easily into the world that lives outside of the ordinary. Many times, our experiences with that place are religious in nature. That is what makes us healers.

Some of us have to learn to be grounded before we can address God in our lives and after we have been to the lost places. But God is still there for us. God is in the quiet places. God is in our hearts. You can ask God for support, and you can find that support in a place that makes sense to you. You can return to the feeling of being safe and loved by God, no matter how far away you have gone. If you have always held onto your relationship with God, through everything, you can make it stronger now that you are in a place where you are more whole. For a long time, I didn't believe in God's love because I felt so broken and alone. But as I took my life back, I also took back my relationship with the divine. When I found myself, I found my connection to God. It had never gone away. It had just gone to a place where I couldn't see it.

When you have done everything you need to do to feel supported inside of yourself and in the world, something beautiful begins to happen. You begin to be a source of support for others. Once you are fully supported, it doesn't have to all be about you anymore. By trusting your inner strength and by connecting with the world around you, you will reach a place where you have everything you need.

When you have everything you need for yourself, you can be a light for others. This is when the magnificence of who you are begins to shine where other people can see it. You have found your roots, and you have begun to feel comfortable on your path. Now your path begins to cross with others' paths.

You will find that all of the things you have done so far to be grounded and supported start having amazing results. You will have a lot more energy available to you, to do what you need to do for yourself and also to do what you are called to do for others. Letting go of layers of fear and heaviness is like lifting a burden off of your shoulders, a burden that you didn't know you were carrying. When you begin to find your sacred self, your life begins to be sacred.

The people and the world around you will respond to you differently once you have cleared off the dirt that was covering the green shoots of your soul. When you find yourself and your place in the world again, no one can take it away from you. You have done the work to uncover yourself and come back from the lost places, and now you have a map of where to go that is inside of you and that you can never lose.

It's like when you go to school and earn a degree. No one can ever take what you learned away from you. Your knowledge is your own, and you can never be without it again. It takes courage to reach out to the world for support. It takes courage to let others into your world. If you feel called to tell your story or tell something about yourself to others as a part of your path, you will have to face feeling vulnerable and afraid. Maybe you will realize, as I did, that you have outdated beliefs that work against you and keep you from feeling and being supported.

The path to change begins inside of you. No one has claim to who you are or what you can do in this life except for you. You can begin following your path, and you can ask absolutely everything and everyone in your life to support you. I recommend that you start by asking for support inside of yourself and then watch quietly as it begins to show up in the people and events around you. You can find the piece of this world that is your own. When you find that place, you cannot be anything but fully supported ever again. The place that is your own is the place you never have to leave. As I have said, it can take a lot of walking and hard work through the broken places and the fears to get there. But your own unlimited support is there in that place, waiting for you.

So begin now to get the support you need. Find something in your life that right now, at this very moment, is supporting you. It can be the chair beneath you that is holding you up from the hard ground. It can be the light above you that enables you to see. It can be your mother in the next room making a delicious-smelling dinner. Something, one thing, lots of things can be supportive in this moment and in all the rest of the moments of your life. Begin to notice the support that keeps you going every day. Embrace that support, and be thankful for it.

Honor the way you are supporting others, too. Notice the way you brought in the trash can so your wife didn't have to. Take a moment and reflect when you hold open the door for a stranger. Give a moment of gratitude when the water from your town's reservoir flows into your bathroom sink so you can brush your teeth before you go to bed.

My path to learning to be supported started with the quiet inside myself and spread out to what I could see and touch. I find a lot of support in the natural world. People were a little harder for me. But as I've unraveled my fears, I've learned to trust them, too.

You can find your own way to know that you are connected to everything, and that, most important, you always have somewhere to turn for who you need to be in this life. You can start on the inside and work your way out. And you will be surprised at what happens when you begin to pay attention. You'll find that everyone and everything rises up to meet you.

Whatever you have come to believe about yourself through the journey you have taken thus far, you can embrace this new truth. You are and will always be a part of this universe, and you are supported by everything. Who you are is much bigger than the smallest thing anyone has ever told you. And who you are is always connected to and loved by the world.

A Space for Beauty and Grace—
Chapter 5—Support Meditation

Gently close your eyes.

Take a deep breath in and center yourself.

Ask the quiet place that is inside of you to support you while you do this meditation.

You are going to go on a journey to see what is supporting you in your life.

First, start with the word.

Support.

Place that word squarely in the center of your heart, where the quiet place lives.

What does that word bring to your mind?

Where do you feel it in your body?

Is there a person or an animal or a place that emerges as you hold the word?

What is right now and always supporting you?

Feel your feet on the floor and the way you are being held by the earth beneath you.

Notice the air swirling around you and coming into you through your breath.

Think of one special way you have been supported lately.

Give thanks for the support that is always available to you.

Ask your quiet place if it has anything else to tell you about support.

Tell it you are open to understanding more about how you are supported in the days and weeks to come.

Give thanks again for the support that keeps you here, where you are walking down your own special path every day.

Take a deep breath in.

Take the word support, and tuck it into your heart.

Slowly open your eyes, and come back to the room.

Remember the support that is always with you.

CHAPTER SIX

Beauty

One of the hardest things about being indefinitely trapped in the locked ward of a psychiatric hospital is the absence of beauty. For me, the state hospital was the worst, with its cinderblock walls, metal beds with cheap plastic mattresses and scratchy linens, and bars on the windows so we couldn't see out or get out. There were even giant heating/cooling machines where the food was prepared before we were each given an orange plastic tray. Salad and pizza somehow heated and cooled together. Strange and completely devoid of beauty. I couldn't even retreat to the bathroom or the privacy of a shower; everything had multiple stalls with curtains instead of doors.

The first time I was in the state psychiatric hospital, a few friends came to visit me, and their visit really brought home to me how ugly my life had become. They were on their way back from a hiking trip in the mountains where they had stayed in a beautiful cabin in the woods. As they sat with me in the airless, windowless visitors' room inside the locked ward, which was the only place I could be, I broke down and cried. I could smell the fresh air on their skin and see the life they brought with them. I could sense the trees and the waterfalls and the mountain views they had just experienced. I couldn't understand how my life had gone so wrong, how these people who had been my best friends and my equals could be free to hike in the sunshine while I was locked in a place that was so ugly and where I couldn't even go outside to get fresh air.

It is hard to believe that you deserve anything beautiful at all or are at all beautiful inside anymore when you are locked away from all the beauty the world has to offer. But even if you have been put in a place where there is no beauty, as I have, you can claim beauty as your own. In fact, it is essential that you do so in order for you to become whole. There is no space between wholeness and beauty. What is whole is always beautiful, and what is beautiful is always whole.

You are beautiful, and you can choose right now to embrace beauty in everything you do and in every part of who you are. You can start with where you are right now. Take a look around. How are you honoring beauty in your life at this very moment? When you look at your surroundings, is there something in sight that makes your heart sing?

We can always take steps that lead us closer to beauty, and eventually our steps will lead us to the place where we can live where we are never separate from beauty, both in ourselves and in the world around us. Our choices to move step by step toward beauty will lead us to our most clear and beautiful selves and then, finally, to our most clear and beautiful lives.

This past year, I made a huge space for beauty in my life by deciding just one thing. After I had done a bit of New Year's cleaning out, I had a huge question for myself. I wondered what it would be like if I only had what I absolutely loved in my house and then, ultimately, because this is the way things work, in my life. My home was already beautiful when I asked myself this question. It was neat and organized and cared-for. But I wanted more. I wanted everything that was taking up space in my home to be something that I loved.

So I began clearing out. There were lots of beautiful things that went on the give-away pile on the dining room table. There were lovely pottery wine glasses that I never used. There were pottery vases that never were the right shape to hold flowers. There were paintings of snow. There were more sentimental things that were harder to let go of, like the bird's nests and dried flowers that I had been collecting for years.

In order to let go of these things that I had lovingly gathered over the years but that no longer served me, I found that I had to be okay with empty spaces for a while. I do most of my home shopping in antique malls and secondhand shops, and to find the things that make my heart sing, I need to spend quite a while looking and passing by the things that are just so-so. I knew that the things I was letting go of weren't easily replaced. But I let them go anyway. And the result is that now everything in my house sings with beauty and love. I feel nurtured and nourished by everything around me when I am in my home.

Feeling nourished gives me energy. I find myself feeling inspired and energized to clean more. I love getting down on my hands and knees with a rag and bucket in hand and cleaning the hardwood floors with my favorite soap. I find that I feel so connected to the bones of the house when I do. I also love dusting the wood furniture with good-smelling natural furniture polish. I even cleaned the blinds to let more sunlight in! When you consciously honor beauty, it begins to honor you, and you will have the energy you need to cultivate more of it.

This clearing out of my house has actually cleared out my life in a lot of ways that are still unfolding. I keep finding myself experiencing more and more beauty. Once you start walking toward beauty, you find all sorts of new beauty that you didn't expect to find.

What steps could you take today to honor beauty in your life? You might have been where I have been, in places where there is so little beauty that a piece of your soul gets broken. But you can get that piece of yourself back. It is waiting for you to notice it and claim it.

Start now. Would you like a special plant next to your bed or a pillowcase with green leaves on it? Can you put the papers that need recycling out on the curb instead of letting them collect on your kitchen table? Can you make the surfaces in your house clutter-free? Start with the space you look at most. What is the view like from your bed? What is the first thing you see when you open your eyes in the morning and the last thing you see at night before you go to sleep? Make that thing beautiful. Make the view from your bed a feast for your eyes and your heart and your soul.

I have a lot of things in my bedroom that have special meaning to me. I have lots of little birds because birds, to me, mean beautiful partnership. I have plants in unusual pottery pots that have interesting shapes. I keep my CDs in a pretty wooden box. I keep my phone charger in a green and brown pottery bowl with a lid. I recently added two tall stems of lucky bamboo because I like to have bamboo in all of my important spaces. I have another bamboo plant beside me on my desk as I write this.

There are lots of other opportunities to cultivate beauty. Pay attention to the food that you eat. Choose foods that are beautiful colors, like red peppers and avocados. Appreciate the perfection of a pear. Let beauty nourish you through everything you put into your body. We have already talked about how we can find support and connection to the food we eat by thinking of how it came to us from nature. Now we can think about its beauty and how that beauty nourishes every cell in our bodies, all the way to our souls.

You can wear beautiful clothes. You can make sure that you feel great in every single thing you wear, and if you don't, you can find another outfit and let that not-so-great one go. Over the past several years, I have bought most of my clothes in thrift shops, but I have made some great finds and found a way to dress that makes me feel beautiful most of the time. I am still working on all of the time. Develop your own style; experiment with what works for you. Don't put anything on your body that makes you feel less than fabulous every day.

Think of beauty in all of its forms, and bring it into your life. What is the most beautiful thing you can think of? What delights you and makes you feel like you're shining, inside and out? Find ways to go toward that thing. The path is open to you. You can go there. Just take the next step.

One of the things I love most is to listen to live acoustic music. I love listening to people playing their guitars and singing. It makes me feel like my heart is opening to the sky. It makes me feel completely alive and free. When I was in the hospital, I wondered when I would be free enough to go hear live music again. It seemed so far away because I knew the only place I could be was in that hospital bed, where the only freedom was to see how still I could lie so I could try to disappear for a little while.

My circumstances after I got out of the hospital for the last time kept me far away from my old life of going to shows with friends. I didn't have those friends anymore. I didn't have any money. I wasn't living where music was available to me. The truth was that, for a long time, I didn't have the light or the energy available to me to even think of music. I was busy just getting myself back.

But eventually I did come back to the place where I could go to see my favorite music with my new friends. The first time I went to see a live show, I cried. It was several years after I had been out of the hospital, but I still remembered that for a time in my life, the thing of beauty that I loved to do the most had been lost to me. And I knew that there were lots of people who were still where I had been before, and live music was something that was very far from their lives. And so were the other beautiful experiences that were to them what music is to me. I feel grateful that I can have so much beauty in my life again, even in the form of music, and I always remember what it felt like to have lost it.

Lately, I have been cultivating good shoes and the perfect bracelet. It starts small, and it gets bigger. Trust that the more beauty you seek, the more resources will become available to give it to you. Beauty loves attention. Your soul wants you to experience beauty because it is a part of being whole. Beauty is like support. It is all around you and inside of you. Now that you know how to find that quiet voice inside of you, ask her what beauty she loves most in the world.

You might love paperweights or photographs of bears. What you love is always yours. Make a decision that you are worthy enough, right now, to have beauty as a companion in every moment of your life. You are beautiful. Have you forgotten? You love to be surrounded by beautiful things, and you love to feel good in your clothes. You love it when your hair is clean and shiny, and you love it when your shoes are not only comfortable but cute!

Maybe you love to be a little sassy and wear skirts with boots, like I do. Do it! Look everywhere until you find what you need to experience your own beauty and the beauty of the world. Beauty has the power to change your life. Don't dismiss the time you spend on a Sunday morning sitting in the park gazing up through the branches of your favorite tree. Begin to notice the power that lives in inside of you as you actually take a moment to go outside of your apartment at night to look up at the full moon.

The clouds and the waterfalls and the hot springs are calling you. The deer that feed at the edge of the forest have a message for you. There is a reason you like to wear purple. It is important that you choose to drink your morning coffee out of the white porcelain cup with the cobalt blue flowers that your grandmother gave you instead of the chipped orange one with the name of the drug company on it.

If you have been in those far-off places we talked about, you might feel that you can't acknowledge that the deer really do have something to say. You might feel hesitant to wear purple because it took on some kind of heightened meaning when you were in that other place, a meaning that didn't quite make sense when you came back.

It doesn't have to make perfect sense. It still has meaning. You still have an inner voice to wholeness that calls to you through what you love—calls that part of you that was never broken. There are parts of that other place that tap into something real inside of you. Remember the sacred calling of your soul. Don't take it all literally. Think of it as a dream. If you dream of turtles every night, it is okay to put a picture of a turtle on your bathroom mirror or to buy a turtle pendant to wear over your heart. If, when you were in that other place, you thought you heard the angels singing to you, it is okay to still believe in angels and to whisper your prayers to your favorite one when you go to bed at night.

When we have been to the places of our soul and told that we are lost, we lose that place in ourselves that went to someplace sacred. You can find that sacred place again by honoring beauty. The divine in you always responds to what you find to be beautiful. You already know what makes you shine. To heal yourself, it is necessary to honor your heart and your soul's callings to you. The way you do this is by going toward what you already love. And you already love what you think is beautiful.

You can also honor beauty by honoring whatever it is that you create from your heart. I like to create beauty with words at this time in my life. In other times, I have liked to make beautiful paintings. Someday I hope to make beautiful pottery. Are you a poet? Do you love to draw? Do you sing as clearly as the stars shine on a brilliant night? Let the beauty of your expression come out into the world. Sing a few notes in the shower. Learn a new song on the violin. Draw that image of a tree you've been seeing. Take a photo of the moss on the bricks on the sidewalk by your door.

When you have been made small by the world, it is hard to remember the bigness that lives inside of you. Especially when some of the bigness was shining through and you were told that was because you were lost. When you have been locked away or pushed down, it is almost impossible to feel beautiful.

Before I went to the hospital, I felt beautiful, and I had lots of beauty in my life. My friends thought of me as a beautiful person. I knew it. I felt it. I believed it. And then suddenly, I wasn't beautiful to them anymore. Not to my family, not to my friends, and not to the doctors. All that they saw when they looked at me was someone who was lost and broken. And so that is what I became in the world. I lost the beauty that had surrounded me, and for a while I lost the beauty that had always lived inside of me.

It actually took me years to remember that, all of the time I felt ugly in the eyes of the people around me, there were still people who saw me as beautiful. In fact, they told me all the time. They said I was beautiful and that they knew I was someone special. They told me that they could see my light.

They were the other patients at the hospitals. They were the people who were just like me, and they were locked away and made small, but they told me I was big. The fact that I forgot the way that they loved me and supported me and saw my bigness even then shows how hard it is to remember the truth of who we are when we are told by the world that we are merely broken and not sacred. The other patients at the hospitals I went to repeatedly told me that I was sacred. They knew that I was doing the work of my soul. But I couldn't hear them until years later because I had been shattered by the people in my world who insisted that I was broken. I knew inside at the time that the experiences I was having were important and sacred, but then I forgot because the consequences of having those experiences in my life were so devastating.

I am telling you what I wish I could have heard from the others like us way back then, before I ever believed that I was lost. I wish I could have known that what they said was true and found a way back to myself much sooner. I wish I didn't have to go to all the hard places you have to go to when you feel alone and ugly in the world. I hope that I am catching you sooner on your path than I caught myself.

You are beautiful. I can see your light. I can see that you have a place and a sacred purpose beyond whatever the world has seen in you so far. I can see that you are right now doing the sacred work of your soul. And I thank you.

Now, go find a way to make your world just a little more beautiful. Keep choosing beauty again and again. Choose it in the smallest ways and in the biggest ones. Choose it, and let it choose you. You deserve it. You are as beautiful as the moonlight over the ocean. You are as beautiful as the tallest tree in the forest. You are simply magnificent. Start letting the world around you reflect it. Choose your own personal path to wholeness. No matter how broken you have felt, you have a light inside of you. Choose that light. Let beauty be your guide.

A Space for Beauty and Grace—
Chapter 6—Cultivating Beauty

There is something for you to do to mend your broken heart. You have to cultivate beauty. I went to a friend's mother's house once. She had lived there for over forty years. But I felt very sad as soon as I walked in. She had nothing in her home of beauty. There were no special vases or colorful paintings or handmade throws over the furniture. There was nothing to show what she loved.

Don't live without beauty in your life for one more minute. Surround yourself with the things that make your heart sing. Begin it now. Do a clearing-out of the things that clutter your life or make you feel unhappy or overwhelmed because they aren't beautiful to you. And then begin the process of allowing beauty in to replace the ugliness. Let only what you love into your life. Start with one space in your house, and create a beautiful sanctuary. You need this sanctuary. Light a candle; buy fresh flowers; put on your favorite music. You deserve beauty in your life. Take a step toward what you love that is beautiful right now. And begin to accept beauty as your right and not something that is held away from you. Make the commitment to beauty and do everything you need to do to honor it. In honoring beauty, you are honoring your heart and your soul at the deepest level.

CHAPTER SEVEN

Purpose

We all know what is ours to do. It is something that has always been with us. I have known I was going to write a book since I was a teenager. I just didn't know it was this book, and, until about a month ago, I didn't know that I would be writing it now. I also always knew that my last name would be my father's name when I wrote the book, even though I went through some name changes since I first thought about writing the book. I knew I would write a book because writing the book is connected to my purpose.

I know that I have a purpose, and I also know now that every single thing that happened in my life to bring me to this moment—the moment when I am sharing that purpose with you—was meaningful. In fact, it was sacred. It has taken me a while to let that in: I am actually a sacred person on a spiritual journey to wholeness. Everything that happens to me matters.

Remember that we are done being broken? Well, in order to be whole, we need to acknowledge who we are. I am not small—and neither are you. My soul is limitless. The beauty and light that I am capable of is only curtailed by how much I allow myself to shine. If you decide that you are going to be your most clear and beautiful self, you can begin the journey that leads you to your own wholeness and light. You can start living from your purpose.

I know about the trips to the hospital and to the mental health clinic. I know about the people coming to your house to bring you your medicine every day at noon and six. I know that you might not have a job that you love, or even a job at all, and that maybe you are trained to be a teacher but have been sitting in your apartment most mornings by yourself until your ride comes to take you to your next appointment.

I know that you might feel heavy and maybe even lost. I know that you might have been so trapped in what other people think of you and what you have learned to think of yourself that it might have been a long, long time since you last allowed yourself to think of your purpose. But it's in there. Just like support and beauty, it is waiting for you to claim it. It is wholly, completely, perfectly, yours.

Start with a word. What is your word? I know you have one. What makes your soul sing? My word is beauty. Everything in my life centers around that one word. Beauty. I am here talking with you about coming back from being lost in what the world calls mental illness, but my real purpose for talking to you is beauty. I know you are beautiful because I know what beauty is. I cultivate it in every aspect of my life. It is what makes my heart beat.

So my true purpose is beauty. As you can see, it can take many forms in the world. For me, beauty is writing and music and mothering and dancing and trees and yoga and walking and my best friend and nourishment. It is everything I can think of that makes me whole and shiny. Really, it is everything I love.

So, what is your word? I am not going to give you any suggestions, other than to ask your quiet place for assistance, if you can't remember your word right now. You know what it is. Give it time to show itself to you. Let it bubble into your heart. Thank it for always being with you. Once you have it, begin living consciously from that word. Honor it in everything you do. Know that your purpose is always tied to that one word, that one wish, that one yearning. There is a meditation at the end of this chapter that might help you.

Now that you have your word, answer this: what is your thing to do that only you can do in the world? Aha! You didn't know I would ask you so fast, did you? You thought you were finished when you remembered your word. Well, the word is just the warm light in the center of your life. You have much more inside of you than just your word.

Let's go back and talk about how we are sacred. It is important. Back when I was in that other place, I went running into the street to get away from a friend who was trying to help me. I held her to the ground because I thought evil was after her. I stood naked in the window of the hospital room. I told people that I was bringing in the light and that there was a battle between good and evil happening right then in the world. I called the police because I thought a woman was being murdered. I asked complete strangers to pray with me. I sang for hours and hours about souls and the light. I was absolutely and completely outside of what normally holds us in the world.

I know that, literally, those things I was saying were not happening in the world where anybody could see them. I know that I needed to come back from that place. I know I couldn't live there. I know that people were right to bring me back for myself and for everyone around me. I really needed to put some clothes on and talk to the doctors and eat something grounding and apologize to my friend.

I really needed to be present for my children and stay out of the hospital and return to normal life. I get it. When we go to that place, we need to come back as soon as we can. But does that mean that place is not sacred? Does the fact that no one was really being murdered mean that everything that happened to me when I went to that place was meaningless? No. I don't believe that. There are common themes for us when we go to that place. These include good and evil and light and darkness. I really was on a healing journey. I really was in the place of my soul.

I really was sacred. The reason I ran out into traffic is not that I was lost. The reason I ran out into traffic is that I was a healer on a healing journey into the unseen worlds of my soul, and I had no one to guide me. I had no one to help me. I had no one to keep me safe and protect me while I undertook my sacred journey. I was all by myself in my house, spinning in the world of the unseen where I had to go so I could come back and be healed, and there was nothing, no one, to ground me and support me. There was no one in my life who could honor me as sacred at that time and watch over me so that I stayed safe until I could come back from that place. The response of the world around me was handcuffs and locked wards and forced medication. No one could see that I was a healer.

Those of us who go to that place are sacred. We are the healers of the world, and we go through our healing journeys all by ourselves. We go to that place because there is magic there. There is something there that heals and transforms what is broken in our world. It is the world of dreams, but we go there when we are awake. This is a sacred task that our souls have undertaken. Once we have gone there, we can come back to the normal world as visionaries and healers. We know that there is power in that place. We can feel it. We are immersed in it. It pulls us so far into it that we can lose our way because we have no guide. We are often the only one in our circle of family and friends who goes there. We go there to heal what is broken so they don't have to. We heal that place in our soul so we can help others heal it in theirs, without having to go to the soul place themselves. We are the gatekeepers to that place.

But we are lost. We are without purpose. We are seen as broken. We see ourselves as the world sees us. We deny our magic. And sometimes, we stay lost. We can't find our way back to ourselves after we have gone to that place because we have forgotten that we are sacred. We do not finish the healing journeys that began when we went to the soul place. We don't claim our place in the world as healers. We don't bring back what we are meant to bring into the world. We don't allow ourselves to be healed so we can heal others as we are meant to.

I have found my place in the world again. I know that I am a healer. I know my purpose. I have remembered that I am sacred. And I have remembered that you are, too. So, back to the question: what is yours to do in this world? What is the thing that only you can do that makes your heart sing and your knees tremble to think about? What is your purpose? You have done the hard part. You have gone to the soul place—and you have come back. You have found yourself again after the world told you that you were lost. You have walked to the place where you know now that you are not small. Who would you be if you let yourself be big?

Your healing journey might not look like mine. And you don't have to do everything that is yours to do today. Your purpose has many facets, and it will take on different faces as you go through your life. Maybe you are meant to be a well-known artist, but right now you need to be a caretaker for your mother. But you can begin it. Start honoring the artist part of you. Do the next thing. What is yours to do now? Once you understand the word that drives you, the next step is to go toward the thing that is yours to do in the world.

You know what is yours to do, just as you knew your word. You already started doing it when you started honoring beauty in your life. Your purpose is tied to what you think is beautiful. You also started fulfilling your purpose the minute you acknowledged that you want to be your most clear and beautiful self. The second you decided you weren't going to be small anymore, you started moving straight in the direction of your purpose. Your inner map activated and put you right on course.

You have already begun to heal all the places inside of you that have been broken. You see now that what you have been through has meaning. You know that your soul is trying to take you somewhere beautiful. You know where you need to walk to get there, and you know about gathering support and honoring beauty along the way.

Now that you have gotten here, your purpose is standing on its head trying to get your attention. It wants to be your guide for everything you do. Your purpose can come to you as a gentle whisper and not as a raging waterfall. You can step into the stream in the calm place.

Our lives are always made up of right now and what is next. All we need to know is the next thing that is ours to do. I knew that I would write a book a long time ago. It took me lots of going from one place to the next to get here, where I am writing it to you. I don't know what is next, what happens after I finish. Except—I do. I know that I will do what I need to do to put the book in the world. And I know that then I will talk to the people who read it. And then I know that my life will center for a time around this book and those people, and then I will write the next book. So I do know. But I don't know exactly when or how or who. I don't know specifically what I will be doing at this exact time a year from now or who will be in my life sharing it with me. And of course there is still the little voice inside of me that says none of it will happen. There is the voice that tries to tell me I will always be small.

But I know that voice isn't right. It's just an old companion that hasn't grown to the places I have grown to yet. So even if you have your old companion that likes to remind you that once you believed you were nothing, you can still begin your journey and take the steps you need to take to be big. You already have.

You will know the next thing that will take you to your purpose because, once you start listening, you can hear it sing to you. It might mean that you have to get out of bed on Sunday morning and go to the coffee house and read the Sunday paper all day. It might mean that you have to go to the bookstore and buy a book about happiness. It might mean that you have to pull together your resume and start looking for a job. It might mean that you need to go to the art store and buy a white journal to write down your dreams.

I knew I was doing my next thing for my purpose when I decided that I was going to tell my story for the first time. I knew it would change my life when I decided I was going to do it, and I was right; it has changed everything. I decided that I was going to talk about my experiences with what people call "hearing voices," even though no one I knew had ever talked about it. I decided that I was going to talk about it to the people in my job, both my coworkers and the people I served. It was scary, but I knew I had to do it to go to the next place. I knew I was called to be seen and not to be hidden away anymore.

My journey has led me through many, many, layers of myself, and I have grown into myself in ways I never could have imagined and yet always somehow expected. It brought me a new job, new people, and new experiences that have only made me stronger and clearer. It has brought me directly along the path to where I am able to be with you now. There is still much, much, more for me to do in my life to fulfill my purpose. I am doing exactly what I have been called to do, yet I feel like I am only at the very beginning of learning who I am when I am living from my soul's purpose.

To get here, I did the work of healing my soul. Then I did the work of grounding myself in the world again. Now I am doing the work of sharing it with others. What is next? I think for me it is beauty. Always, everything beautiful. I hadn't traveled for ten years, but last fall, I went to California. I smelled the magnolia trees and watched the whales feeding in Monterey Bay. There is much more beauty like that in my life to come. I am at the threshold of my most clear and beautiful life. I can feel it, and I can see it. Now I just need to walk through it. And I am doing that, right now, here, with you.

There is so much loveliness available to us. I know that we have been shattered. But when we pull ourselves back together again, there is so much more for us to do than be ill and broken. Your wholeness is calling out to you right now and always.

You already thought about the most beautiful thing you could think of, and you took the steps you needed to take toward that. Now, get quiet for a moment and think of the most sacred thing you can think of. What is it and how is it tied to you? What calls to you over and over again, like the wind whispering through the leaves of the trees? What does the wind say to you when you open your heart and listen?

Who are you in your most sacred self? What was your soul trying to tell you when you went to that other place? What were you meant to bring back for the rest of us? Feel the power in your belly. Connect to your roots. What comes up through them that needs to be shared?

What is the sacred purpose of your soul? Does it have a name? Does it come with a feeling? Does it have a type of person or a plant or and animal that is connected to it? Once you have opened yourself to the truth of who you are, you can never go back. You don't have to. Where you were before is no longer yours. All that is yours is where you are now. You can learn from where you have been, and you can always remember—but it is time for you to stop being stuck there. It is time for you to acknowledge where you are now. It is time for you to honor your calling and your light.

Your life has brought you here for a reason. Ask your quiet place what that reason is. Stop dismissing where you have been as lost, and start admitting that you have always been heading to someplace beautiful. Now, claim your beautiful place. Claim the place of your sacred self. Claim your light and your calling. You are here. You are supported. You are beautiful. And you are sacred. It is time for you to be whole. It is time for you to acknowledge your purpose.

A Space for Beauty and Grace—
Chapter 7—Your Sacred Purpose Meditation

Sit quietly with your feet on the floor.

Close your eyes.

Take a deep breath in, and let it go.

Imagine yourself walking down the path that leads to your beautiful place.

You are going to the place that you went to before, when you asked about your purpose.

Feel yourself arriving in that place.

Notice the scenery around you.

Acknowledge the beauty of this special place, and take a moment to relax and breathe in the joy of being here.

As you stand in this place of beauty, ask yourself a question.

Ask the quiet place inside of you that knows everything what you need to know now about your purpose.

What is your sacred calling?

Let what comes settle into your heart.

What is yours to do that only you can create in the world?

Call to mind the word that is the center of your life and means everything to you.

Let the word make a picture in your mind.

What does your word have to tell you about your purpose?

Does it have a smell or a taste or a feeling associated with it?

What power lives inside of you to do what is yours to do?

Really let your power of purpose go deeply into your heart.

Feel it pulsing through your body with each beat of your heart.

Feel it filling you with its light and strength.

Take a deep breath in, and let it become a conscious part of you.

Now, ask yourself what you can take back to your life from this place, what will help you remember who you really are?

Take that word or phrase or object and tuck it away inside a safe place where you can find it whenever you need it.

Thank your inner wisdom for supporting you.

Take a last look at the beauty that surrounds you in this special place.

Know that it is always with you and that you can return to it at any time.

It is your powerful place.

Begin walking back down the path that led you here.

Walk slowly and comfortably, knowing that you are clearer than when you came.

Keep walking until you feel yourself back where you came from.

Take a deep breath, and slowly come back to the room.

Open your eyes as you feel ready.

CHAPTER EIGHT

Strength

You have to be strong to be whole and fulfill your purpose. Or rather, I should say that you are going to have to find the strength that is already inside of you and pull it out to put it in the place where you can see and recognize it for what it is. You are going have to make friends with your strength. Your strength is right there inside of you, waiting for you to notice the curve of her face and the touch of her hand. She comes to you all the time, when you are awake and in your dreams. She is your constant companion. She is the line in you that never gets crossed.

A beautiful, wise grandmother that I know likes to call herself resilient. I do love the way that word sounds. Those of us who have been to the lost places are not only strong, we are resilient. It is necessary for us to see this in ourselves and to know how incredibly strong and resilient we are in our center. In fact, it is crucial.

Once you start looking, you will find that your strength is a friend who is easy for you to talk to. You wouldn't be here right now without her. Let her begin to talk with you. What does your strength look like? What does she feel like? My strength is tall and quiet like an oak tree. My strength is firmly planted by her roots, deep into the earth, yet she knows how to sway gently in the wind and the rain. She knows how to feel the sunshine on her branches, and she knows how to stand in one place and let everything she needs come to her. I know my strength well, and I can always feel her around me. I live inside of her every day.

Is your strength a tree like mine? Or is it a mountain? Can you picture your strength as an eagle soaring high above the ground and seeing everything spread out in loveliness beneath her? Are you strong like the ocean or like a waterfall? One woman I asked this question of discovered that her strength was gentleness. Like the gentleness of a mother duck with her babies, floating on a green pond on a warm, sunny day. Your special strength is calling to you. Right now. Can you stop and listen to her?

I first found my strength again after I had been lost to it the way I first found my spirit: through connecting with nature. I connected to nature physically through walking and noticing it all around me. And then I connected with it through prayer and meditation.

When we are told we are broken and that is how the world sees us, it might be very hard for us to connect fully with our strength. Sometimes, when we have been trapped in the world of mental illness, it is hard for us to remember who we are beyond that role of the ill person.

Maybe you are identified as the person in your family or at your job or with your care providers as the person who always needs help and never contributes anything. It is easy to fall into that role, especially if you have been in the hospital, where it can feel like there is really nothing for you to do to contribute to the world except do your best to get to a place where they let you out of there.

Maybe you and others see the people around you as contributing something, but you are just the one who is getting help. Sometimes we are in a place where this is necessary. We all need help sometimes, and we all have places in our life where we are working so hard on ourselves that we are not giving as much as others to the world around us. But this is a temporary time in our lives. Or it is meant to be. We need to not let ourselves get stuck there. You have something special and unique to contribute to this world. We cannot all do what we need to do without you doing your part. You are as unique and necessary and magnificent as your psychiatrist or your case manager or your mother or your brother. You are someone with a purpose, just like them.

We have talked about you discovering your purpose. You already know what it is, or at least you have a glimmer or know what is next. You have opened your heart to it, so it is on its way to you. Now let's honor it by seeing our strength.

I can write. I can make beautiful salads. I am good with computers. I listen very well, and people trust me. These are some of my strengths. What are yours? Are you good with animals? Do you like to build things? Are you an artist or a musician?

What have you been doing lately in your life that you know you are good at? Have you let that slip away from you because you have been consumed by being one of the broken ones? Have you covered up your strength and gotten to a place where all you think about or identify with is the other place and the fact that you have gone there and had a hard time coming back? Have you given up on yourself and who you know you are?

Part of being grounded in this world again is being fully yourself. If you are an artist at heart, you need to paint. If you can't paint, you need to pick up a pencil and draw. If that's too hard, you need to hang a poster of your favorite painting above your bed. If your strength is being an artist but you have forgotten because you have been too lost, you need to honor that strength and bring it back into your life. You don't have to do everything right now. But you have to do something right now to start. And you can begin to honor that strength because it is your strength. It is yours and always has been. It is waiting for you to claim it.

For a long time, I have had a habit of giving my life away to other people. When I have an idea or want something, I have long thought that it was in someone else's hands to give it to me. It was a way of being powerless and a way that I have denied my strength. I can still catch myself doing it. For instance, I want to do better in my life financially. I don't want to have just enough or not quite enough money every month. I want to have more than enough. I want to be able to take my children on vacations to beautiful places. We haven't done that because there just hasn't been extra money. I want to have a big savings account. I want to be at ease and not always struggling.

But I have felt powerless about changing that in my life. I haven't known how to do it. And I think it's up to someone else to create it for me. My boss needs to give me a raise, but I know he never will because it doesn't work that way. God needs to intervene and drop a mysterious $30,000 check in my lap unexpectedly. I have been putting it outside of myself and not taking it into my own hands. I have not been relying on my own strength to give me what I want and take me where I need to go.

It has helped me to look at other people who already have what I want in my life. There is a woman in my dance class who wears beautiful, expensive clothes that I admire, and she goes to France to see her boyfriend. At first I looked at her with envy. But I realized it wasn't jealously or envy that I needed to focus on. It was the fact that I somehow thought I was different from her. I somehow was denying my strength and what was possible for me in the world. I thought that people who can afford nice clothes and go to France for their vacation are somehow different and better than me. I thought there were limits to my life that others didn't have because they were special in a way that I was not. That was me being powerless.

The woman with the expensive palazzo pants and the boyfriend in France is just like me. She is beautiful and strong, and she is doing what is hers to do in the world. Maybe she is a little farther along the path in those areas than I am. But she and I have the same potential. When we acknowledge our strength and decide to live from it every day, our world changes. Our strength is what leads us to what we need and want. When we do what is truly ours to do, everything gathers around us to support us. I am right at this moment doing what is mine to do by writing this book. What I am sharing with you is my strength, and that strength and my willingness to share it in the way that I am called to is my path to my most clear and beautiful life. It is my entryway into beautiful boutique, wide-legged pants and trips to the hot springs in California.

Those things might not be important to you; maybe you don't want more money or to travel to stunning places in the world like I do. But I know there is something beautiful, something that would make you feel free, something that you do not have in your life right now and that is calling to you. And the way you respond to its call is by acknowledging your strength and moving toward it. Step by step.

There is something inside of you that can never be taken away or diminished, no matter what you have been through or how the world sees you. And you have an inner map that will take you directly to it. It is the strength that you were born with and that you have carried with you all along. It is aching for you to notice it.

If you are one of the ones who live every day with the darkness that the other place can hold, through hurtful voices and states of fear and terror or sadness, you have more strength than anyone. You are one of the strongest healers this world has. I know the people around you don't see you that way. But it is the truth. You are in a place that only healing warriors like yourself are strong enough to live in and return from.

Your strength is much greater than the darkness that exists in that other place. Once you know who you are, you can begin to come out of that world. When you recognize that you are a healer and a protector of the light, you can begin to take the path that leads out of that place where you are always dealing with the darkness that the rest of us can't see.

You are a powerful healer, and your light protects the rest of us. There is more for you to do than being trapped in the other world. I was in that world, and I know how terrifying or numbing it can be. But there is a path out of it. The path is open to you, now that you know you had a purpose for being there. You know the way out. Your strength will hold you and lead you out of that place. The whole world around you is supporting you now. We are in a time in the world where there is much more support than there used to be. Those of us who have been to the lost places can come out much sooner now. Those of us who still go there don't have to stay there as long.

Call on your strength to support you. Make the decision and the commitment to yourself that you are going to claim your most clear and beautiful life for yourself right now. Begin to find ways every day to honor your strength.

I had someone tell me recently that he has lost all faith. He says he has nothing to believe in, and that lack of faith keeps him in the world of that other place where he is terrified and there is only darkness. He said he has to believe in something, but he has nothing because that dark world is too strong. He is trying to believe in his favorite T-shirt because he needs to hold onto to something.

I told him that I found my way out of that place where I believed in nothing and felt completely alone and lost by starting with something that was easy for me to believe in, which was a tree. God seemed much too scary and far away, and a tree was just so real and visible and comforting. It was something I could believe in because I could see it and touch it and smell it and feel it.

He said he had always liked hawks. I encouraged him to start with believing in a hawk. Now is the time for you to call on the strength of that thing that you have always loved. Your strength is in what you love in the world, and it is in what you love to do. It is and always has been yours. It is what always brings you hope, or a smile, or a light, or a sense of safety.

Remember, I said it is the line in you that never gets crossed. We all have that line. Even if we've been abused, or terrorized, or made a victim. Even if the thing that terrorizes us is right inside our own head. Even if we are one of the ones that has acted strangely to others because of what that place has told us to do. No matter how much the darkness or the strangeness of that other place has tormented you, there is something in you that it has never touched.

You can touch it now. You can hold it and let it hold you. Nothing can ever break you, because you are too strong and resilient to let it. Your strength is actually apparent in the world that you are a part of. You can call the strength inside of you that is a part of the world by whatever name means the most to you. It might help to think of it as an oak tree or a hawk. It might be in your joy in your grandson's pride when he learns his first word. It might start in your faith in God. There is something that calls to you, something that you have faith in, something that represents your strength.

Once you have begun to understand how your strength is reflected in the world, you must begin to acknowledge the many strengths inside of yourself. There are many things that you are really good at. It is time to bring them back into your life and into the world around you. It is time to offer yourself in service to the world. For example, if you make the best macaroni and cheese in your family, you can decide to make a special dish of it and take it to your cousin's birthday party. Maybe it has been so long since you shared anything of your strength that your family forgot that you can cook at all. But now that you have remembered that your strength is your constant friend, you can decide to show your family who you are again.

It is time to stop hiding your strength. It is time for you to be who you really are. For a while now, I have been hiding out in the world as an ordinary person. I was glad to be ordinary because I remembered what it felt like to be seen as less than even what a normal person was seen as. After I went to the hospital, I wasn't even ordinary; I was just seen as broken and ill. Ordinary was a step up for me.

But now ordinary isn't enough anymore; my strength told me that I have more to do. I have to tell you who I am so you can see who you are. I have to step out of the shadows and into the world where people can see me. That is not a very easy thing to do. At least not for me. But a part of my strength is that I will always remember where I have been and how I came to the place where I can stand in the light. I will always know what it feels like to be less than ordinary. I will always know what it is like when the world sees you as broken. And now that I am not broken anymore, I can see that for the gift it is. No matter what happens to me from now on or where my path takes me, I will never lose the strength of knowing who I am.

Your strength will take you to the place where you are always in the light, just like mine has. It will always talk to you and tell you what you need to do next. All you need to do is listen. It might start as a whisper. It might start with something as simple as thinking about the oak tree in the park or your daughter's smile when you feel lost. But it has a voice inside of you that can get loud enough so you can always hear it, and it will hold you close if you let it.

You are not only magnificent; you are not only a healer and a seeker of beauty and a person who has a purpose. You are someone who is deeply, incredibly strong. Your strength is like the ocean. Your strength is as fluid and beautiful as a waterfall. You are the eagle soaring high above the ground with clear eyes and sturdy wings.

You can rely on something that is inside of you to take you exactly where you need to go. You can rely on your strength. Remember, you are fully supported. The world around you is holding you in a place where you can't be broken. And so is your strength. Let go now of what has kept you feeling broken. It is time. The truth isn't about what has been wrong with you. The truth is about what has always been right. The truth is about your strength.

A Space for Beauty and Grace—
Chapter 8—Strength Meditation

Place your feet on the floor.

Close your eyes.

Take a deep breath in.

You are going to ask the quiet place about your strength.

Put your hands gently over your heart.

Notice the quiet place that lives there.

Take another breath, and let the quiet fill you.

Feel your heart beating, and feel your breath in your chest and your belly.

Feel the pulsing aliveness that fills your body.

Now find your strength.

What does your strength want to say to you?

What image or word or feeling comes to mind?

What would happen if you called on your strength to support you and take you everywhere you need to go?

What would you be like if you were always aware of your strength?

What thing in nature or in the world represents your strength?

Let your strength talk to you for a minute.

Listen closely to what it has to say.

Tuck its message into the quiet place that lives in your heart.

Tell your strength that you will begin to honor it and ask it to support you.

Now take a deep breath in.

Slowly open your eyes, and come back to the room, knowing that your strength is returning with you.

CHAPTER NINE

Acceptance

We have talked a lot about who you are and how you may have forgotten the truth of your own magnificence. It is entirely possible that you have been spinning around a long time in situations that make you small, as I was, and that you have completely misplaced who you are in your most clear and beautiful self. Maybe you never have known that you actually are clear and beautiful and brilliant. And maybe the world around you has told you again and again, as it told me, that you are not anyone special. Maybe the world has convinced you that you are not and never will be a sacred healer with a unique and necessary purpose that no one else can fulfill but you.

Have we come far enough together that you can see that your smallness is not the most essential part of yourself? Have you understood enough in our journey so far that you can see that, however ill you have been, there is much more for you to do? Can you see that, even if you have been very, very lost like I was, there is always a place waiting for you where you are completely found?

It's a hard thing to accept our magnificence in a world that tells us we are broken and lost. The world seems to do everything it can, after we have been to the lost places, to keep us small and powerless. But it is necessary for all of us who have been to the place called mental illness to find ourselves again and to return to the truth of who we are. This is true of every human being on the planet. We all need to find ourselves again and return to the truth of who we are. But somehow, those of us who have been to that other place called mental illness are told we don't have that same essential drive from our soul to do what is ours to do in the world anymore. Once we have been lost, it is understood that we will just stay there. We become about getting through and lose the part of us that is about healing the world.

The world needs to be healed. Now more than ever. Each one of is crucial to all the others. The people in your life can't do what they need to do unless you do your part. They especially need you because you understand the world in a way that they can't. You have been to the places of the soul that not everyone goes to. You are now and always have been on a special healing mission.

That might sound absurd; after all, when you are in that other place and you tell people that exact thing, that you are on a special healing mission, they respond by telling you that you are delusional and that you need to get yourself back to normal as quickly as possible.

I know all about the locked wards and the forced medication that come when you tell people that you are talking to God or that you are a healer. But their response does not mean that they know the truth and that you are grandiose and that you are not a healer; their response is what it is because, when you are in that other place, you are not making sense to the ordinary world. When you are in that other place, you might not be taking care of yourself the way you need to, or you might be doing things that appear very strange and unbalanced.

You really are a healer. You really are having visions and experiencing deep understanding of things that matter. But when you are there, in that other place, you are not yet where you can share it with others or have it make sense in this world. That place really is a lost place, no matter how sacred it is or how necessary it is that you go there.

So, the truth is that you are a healer. Your journey is sacred. You do have a direct connection with God. That is true for all of us. Those of us who go to the place that is called mental illness are no different. In fact, in some ways, we can be even more connected to our sacredness and the sacredness of the world.

When you have done everything you need to do to come back from that sacred place that is also the lost place, as I have, you can start to tell people about what you know. But first, you have to come back. It is true that no one listens to you when you are still there. It is true that you need to start walking toward wholeness again after you have been there. You need to pay your bills and buy groceries and care for what you need to care for so that you can fulfill your sacred purpose. This is just as important to your life as the fact that you went to that place. And after you have gotten good at caring for your physical life, you have to get good at caring for your soul and your spiritual life. You need to find your inner sparkle. Not from that other place but from a place that is grounded and rooted in this world. You need to seek out support and beauty, and you need to discover your purpose and your strength.

And after you have done all of the things we have talked about, you need to do another thing. And this thing might be harder than going for a walk and painting a beautiful picture of an eagle and telling your mother the bravest thing you have to tell her from your heart. This thing that you have to do might make you want to turn back and try to remember how to lie still on your bed and disappear for a while. But the truth is, you can't go back. Not now. It is too important to all of us that you keep walking.

The thing that you have to do to fulfill your sacred purpose is here with you right now as you read this. You have to be willing to do what is yours to do. And in order to do that, you have to stop being small. You have to be willing to be magnificent. You have to be willing to see your magnificence for yourself in your very own heart. It is not up to me to tell you about it anymore. You have to see it for yourself. You have to accept your own greatness.

Your own greatness is your path to the healed life that you have always been meant to live. I have been holding it for you. Now it is time for you to hold it for yourself. Ask your quiet place about it. See what is has to say to you.

For me, accepting my greatness meant that I had to let go entirely of what other people thought about me. No one believed me when I was in the soul place, and I told them that I was on a healing journey. They told me that I was grandiose and that I couldn't possibly be a healer. In fact, they did everything they could to make sure I didn't believe it either.

It took me many years to come back to my truest self because I had been so pushed down by the world's response to me. It has only been through helping other people and being willing to face every fear that has showed up and do everything that I have been called to do that I can tell you now that I know my own truth. I have accepted that I truly am a healer, after a long time of struggling to do so. I can embrace my own healer self because I have arrived in the place where I can see how my own acceptance of being a healer brings a light to others who have been in the same places that I have been. I can see that I have found a way of coming out of the lost places, and, in doing that, I have become exactly who I said I would be when I was in those places. I am a person who knows about the places of the soul and about healing from those places, and I also know how to heal from the consequences in our world of going there.

What do you need to do to accept your own magnificence? What is the quiet place telling you about the truth of who you are? Don't be afraid that if you accept your own magnificence you will lose your ability to be humble. Once we have been made small by the world and lost what we have loved, we never forget how to be humble, no matter how well the world begins to treat us.

The world treats me pretty well these days. People admire the position I am in. But I will never, ever forget where I have been. And I can honestly say that I am thankful now for all of it. It brought me here to you. And most important—it brought me to myself. Accepting your light does not take you away from other people who need you. It takes you directly to them.

When you have finally accepted your magnificence, the world around you can finally respond to you in the way you need it to. The truth is, we have to do our inner work first before the outer world will respond. Because you are one of the ones whose soul was chosen to go to the sacred places, you have unlimited potential for healing and light. Your strength and your beauty are infinite. You are a healer on a healing journey, so of course you are meant to be healed. Yet, you can do nothing to heal others without first healing yourself.

Accepting yourself as a healer is the first step to your own healing. We have talked about that a lot. We already understand that we are healers. Accepting our magnificence comes next and is our key to freedom. I am much freer now than I have ever been in my whole life. I am free because I know what is mine to do. I know what is mine to do because I know who I am. I know who I am because I uncovered myself step by step. The green shoots of my soul are fully rooted in the earth but also completely available to the sunlight and the raindrops. I am in the place now where there are unexpected rainbows and soft, gentle breezes that caress my leaves. You can be in that place, too.

What do you understand about your magnificence? Really go deep and remember who you are. Your magnificence has always been with you. It has called to you your whole life. It has always been your companion, just like your strength. It has been waiting for a long time for you to acknowledge it.

If you are like me, you have layers and layers of all of that murky fear that we talked about earlier to go through to get to the place where your magnificence can shine freely.

It's not just fear; it's also old stuff. Things people have said to you, beliefs you have held onto. Experiences you have had that have hurt you throughout your whole life. All the parts of you that only serve to keep you small and hold you back. You don't need those parts anymore. You might not be able to let them all go in one day. But you can begin to unravel them, layer by layer. The murkiness that keeps you small is no longer necessary. You know who you are now. Nothing can take you from your path.

Our murkiness serves a purpose, but we reach a point where we need to brush it off and let our true light shine through. I am at a place now where I don't have to be murky any more. Things still show up. But I work through them. And I release them. I release them through writing in my journal and talking with friends and praying and dancing. One of my favorite ways to release them is by writing them down and giving them to the fire. There are all kinds of ways to uncover who you really are.

Find your way. Draw. Paint. Write. Sing. Dance. Do whatever your creative self tells you to do. Inside of your magnificence is your most creative self. You are a poet or a teacher or songwriter or a fabulous chef. I know you have a creative part of you that longs to be expressed. Accepting your own light means letting that part of you shine freely.

And once you uncover it for yourself, it is time to let it show to others. We could sit in our houses alone all the time and never share our light with anyone, but really, why would we? If we did, we would be missing the whole point. This life is about connecting with other people. You need to show the world who you are. The world absolutely needs you. You are essential to every person in your life. And you have a message and a purpose that will help others who can't get where they need to go without being touched by you. It doesn't matter if you are a magnificent healer if you never share what you have learned about yourself and your journey and if you keep yourself hidden from the world. It is time to stop hiding!

First you had to stop hiding your magnificence from yourself. And that might have been kind of hard. It was for me. But you have done it. Or at least you have begun. For the first time in a long time or maybe ever, you are at a place where you can step into your life as your most magnificent self. And you are completely supported by your highest self and the world around you in doing that. You are strong and clear and beautiful. And now you are able to recognize it. If you still can't see yourself for who you truly are, keep unraveling those layers. Keep sloughing off the murkiness. Keep your intention of finding and living from your own light. You will get there. Keep remembering your strength and your purpose. Keep seeking beauty. Just keep walking down your path.

Who are you in service to others? We know you are a healer. But what is yours to heal? Why did your soul choose you to go down this path where, for a while, you seemed lost and broken to the world? Why did you have a time in your life where you felt less than magnificent? Why did you go to the soul place at all? What did you need to bring back? And now that you are back, what is yours to do that no one else can do?

You know that you are responsible for who you are. Right? We have gotten that far. And you know that everything you have been through has a purpose. You no longer have to be a victim of what others have done to you or how you have been treated. Whatever happened to you may have been very, very hard. It might have knocked you down and taken away your breath. But you are here now. You have arrived in a different place. And this is the place where you can make your life your own.

So what is yours to share with others? It might be tempting to hold onto what you heard and felt in that other place in a literal way. Maybe there was something about good and evil or God and the devil. Maybe there was some huge plan at work that only you could see. Let that go for now. That might be important, but it is not your work in the world. Your work in the world is about you and who you are in your most clear and beautiful self. Your work in the world is about your heart and everything that you love, both small and large.

Your work in the world is about you being grounded right here and right now. You need to be present with what is all around you. You need to show your beautiful light to others. In order to do that, you have to first see your beautiful light for yourself.

That is what we have been talking about all along. That is what I have been trying to tell you. Look inside yourself, and see yourself for who you really are. That is your purpose. And when you are fully grounded, fully present with the magnificence that lives there, you can begin to be who you need to be for others.

What you have been through was necessary. Your family and your friends needed you to be exactly who you have been for their own healing and light. Even the hard parts have been necessary. But you don't have to stay in the hard places any more. You can come out into the light of your own soul. And you can show the people who love you that you are strong and beautiful and that they can trust you. You can show them that you have something special to offer. You can stop being one of the broken ones and start being who you really are, which is someone who knows what it means to be whole.

The truth is that you are whole and you always have been. The truth is that you are magnificent and very, very beautiful. You are a light that needs to be seen. You are a gift to the world. You are a hero who has been on a magical journey to wholeness. It is time for you to accept yourself for who you truly are. I know it has been hard. But the worst is behind us. Once we know who we are, nothing can take our light away from us. Nothing even wants to. When we have claimed our light and have begun to share it with others, we are doing what is ours to do. And when we are doing what is ours, the universe rises up to meet us.

You can begin it right now. In fact, you already have. I honor you. Thank you for seeing your own magnificence. You have come a long way in healing the world.

A Space for Beauty and Grace—
Chapter 9—Magnificence Meditation

You can put your feet on the floor.

Or you might want to try this meditation lying down on your back in a comfortable position.

Take a deep breath in.

Notice the sensations in your body.

Check in with your quiet place.

Take another breath in, and let go of all thoughts and cares of the day.

Focus on being right here, right now.

It is time for you to acknowledge your magnificence.

What does your quiet place have to tell you about your magnificence?

Place your hands over your heart.

This is where your quiet place lives.

It is also the place where your magnificence lives.

Feel your heart opening and expanding to the brilliance of who you really are.

What does your true magnificence look like? What does it feel like?

Take a moment to really let it in.

Take a moment to feel held by the world around you and supported in being who you are from your own unique magnificence.

Make a commitment to yourself and the world that you will honor this essential part of you.

Make a commitment to be whole.

Ask your heart if it has anything else to tell you.

Now hold what you have learned in a place where you can always find it and return to it.

Take a few deep breaths in, and slowly come back to the room.

Know that you are ready to be who you have always been meant to be.

CHAPTER TEN

Faith

You can see now that you have something important that you need to do for yourself and to offer to the world. You have begun to accept what is yours to do, and you have touched the seed of your own magnificence, which lives in your heart. We have done a lot of work uncovering who you are in your most clear and beautiful self.

What do you believe in that is bigger than your own soul and your own heart? Where do you put your faith? It is true that you are magnificent. But you are not magnificent alone. There is something bigger than you that holds you and supports you and shows you where you need to go. There is a presence inside of you right now that is working with you to bring you the love and light that you deserve. There is a divine spark in you that is supporting you in fulfilling your purpose.

When we are afraid and when we think we are nothing, we are not honoring the truth of the divine spark that lives inside of us. The other day, my dear friend was very upset about something that was happening at home. I listened to him. And then I told him what I believed was true. I told him that he would be okay. Because I knew he would be. He got very, very angry with me.

Sometimes that happens with me. These days, I tend to have a positive attitude about everything. I believe that the goodness and the light always win because, in truth, they always do. But people who are in places where they feel hopeless and lost sometimes don't like to hear that something good will happen to them ever again. My friend wanted me to listen, but he wasn't ready to move out of the place where his feelings of anger and hopelessness were taking him.

Right then, he wanted to stay lost in his fear that his world was coming to an end and he would lose everything he cared about. He was feeling powerless and angry and afraid. What he was lacking in that moment when he was spinning around in his powerlessness and fear was faith. When we feel lost we don't want to ask God to help us. We don't want to trust in the light inside of us. We want to focus on staying lost.

I understand where my friend was living in that moment when he was powerless and angry and afraid. I have been there, too. When I was first struggling to get my life back I didn't feel any faith in something bigger than myself. I was just doing what I needed to do to regain what I had lost, and I was actually afraid of God. For a long time, I believed that God was scary and that the universe didn't care about me or what happened to me. I didn't understand how God could have let such hard things happen to me. I couldn't see that everything in my life had a purpose that was leading me here to you.

When I started finding myself again, I also had to find my faith in something bigger than myself. I've already talked to you a lot about how I started regaining my strength and my faith through trusting in the natural world and sending up my prayers through my favorite tree. I knew the tree wasn't the one that was answering my prayers, though. I knew what I was really doing was letting myself connect again to God.

For a long time my only prayer was, "May I feel God's love in my heart." In fact, I held that prayer with me for many years. I didn't feel like that prayer was really being answered, but now I see that it was. I had to get through the layers of murkiness that were between myself and my connection with the divine to actually feel God in my heart again.

When we feel sad or angry or lost, it is easy to want to spin in those feelings and deny that there is anything loving or positive to hold onto. We can go into our darkness and resist anything that tries to bring us out. It is easy to feel hopeless and alone. We can feel like we are uniquely powerless, nothing is supporting us, and everything is working against us.

Another friend likes to say that he feels like he is in a no-win situation in his job and in his life. But, actually, I don't believe him. There is always a way out of the darkness. He has a way out of his. He is just afraid to do what he has to do to free himself. He doesn't know how to trust in his own power or to believe in something bigger than himself. There is always something we can do to connect with the powerful love that lives in our hearts. God is always quietly waiting for us to acknowledge the truth of the divine presence inside of us. We are always supported in moving toward the light.

I have had to come to an understanding of God in the same way I had to find support and honor beauty and acknowledge my strength and my purpose. I have had to face my fear and do what was next and really make a commitment to going toward the light. Fear comes up still and wants to hold me away from the truth of God in my heart and my life, but I don't let it stay for very long.

When we are lost, we need to activate our inner maps to take us to the place where we are found. And we can't do that without faith. You don't have to believe in God the same way I do or the same way the other people in your life do. But in order to be whole, you do need to have faith in something bigger than yourself.

I did an experiment recently when I was away from home, in an environment where the people I was with didn't have a lot of faith in the things I believe in. In fact, I don't think they would understand me much at all if I showed them what I believe in my heart. My experiment was to see what would happen if I removed all of my faith and hope in the future and my belief in something bigger than myself. I wrote in my journal about what could be possible if I didn't believe in the magic of the divine at all. It was eye-opening. It got me into a bad place that I recognized as a place that some of the people of my life actually live in all the time. It showed me that I never want to go back to a place where I don't have faith. It showed me how precious and crucial to my life my faith is. I realized that I can go nowhere in my life that I need to go without my belief in goodness and light. I realized that my faith is necessary for me to fulfill my purpose. And I realized that all of the magical things that happen when you trust in goodness are optional. You can choose not to let them in.

I am where I am today because I did the work of getting here. I faced my fear again and again and did whatever the next thing was that I was called to do. When other people were standing still, I was walking. I stood still for a while myself. But then I recognized that was what I was doing and chose to move forward, and that has made all of the difference in my life. Now, because good things are happening to me, people can think that it is easy for me and make me into someone who is different from them. Somehow, I have become one of the ones who somehow has it easy and is set apart from the pain that others experience.

It's not true. I still understand the pain, even though I don't live in it anymore. I had to go through it, too. We all do. It is what makes us human. The only difference between me and the people who are still stuck and feeling powerless is that I have walked through that place on the path and come through it. And when that place tries to call me back, I don't let it, at least not for very long. I rely on my faith to take me to the place of goodness. It is a choice that I continue to make, again and again. When I am feeling afraid that the world will try to hurt me, I remember that God is love. When something happens that makes me feel overwhelmed or powerless, I face it directly in the eye and do what I need to do to find my power inside of it. When I feel small and lost, I consciously choose to tune in to the quiet place inside of me where God lives and to remember what is true about myself and my situation from that place. And I am always willing to ask God for help.

I acknowledge that my power is not wholly my own. I am the keeper of my strength and my light, but I have faith in the divine presence that lives in my heart. You have a quiet place inside of you where God lives. We all do. It doesn't matter how you define that place. What matters is that you recognize it and go to it when you need help.

By tuning into the quiet place, we can find the answers to what we need to do to be our most clear and beautiful selves. We can learn to cultivate that quiet place inside of us. What I know that my friend was forgetting when he was spinning around in his fear is that I am not alone. I always know this now. I have gotten to a place where I never forget it. So, when things get hard, I find comfort and guidance from God. And that is always more loving and helpful than being afraid that the worst thing I can imagine happening is always looming in front of me.

The truth is, most of the time we have what we need right now. If we are homeless and it is cold and we are hungry, we might need a blanket or shelter or food and not have it. But that is not what most of us are living like right in this moment. Do you have what you need right now? I mean really? I could use more money or a partner or to fit in the clothes I want to wear again, but actually, in this very moment, there is nothing that I need that I don't have. Where we get in trouble is in thinking that we won't have what we need in the future. We are afraid we will go back to the hospital or lose our job or not have enough money to pay the rent. That is where our faith can come in to support us.

Just like the world around us is always supporting us, so is the world of God inside of us. We are always supported. We just have to come to the place where we believe that this is the truth. We are faced again and again with the choice between fear and faith. When we are in the place of fear, it is easy to believe that that is all there is. But it is not true. We do have a choice. Always, in every moment, we have a choice.

What keeps us stuck is that we are more comfortable, sometimes, in the pain we are familiar with than the pain we imagine will come to us in the future if we let go of our fear and follow our faith. Our fear says it is trying to protect us, but really, it is a wall between ourselves and our most clear and beautiful lives—a wall that we have to have the courage to climb over.

You might be wondering how this applies to everything we have already talked about. How your magnificence and your faith intersect. The truth is that they are married to each other. They are partners that will never separate. You are not magnificent on your own; you are magnificent because you have the divine inside of you. What we have been doing on our journey together thus far is uncovering that divine spark that makes you who you are. You are not magnificent because of what you are afraid of; you are magnificent because of what you believe in and what you love.

If you are still feeling far away from your faith, start with what you love. God is always in what we love. Just like beauty and purpose and strength are. Your inner map to being found always starts with what you love. Let that be your guide to the divine. And let yourself believe in magic. Don't think you have to remain true to what your fear tells you. Don't think you are protecting yourself by always imagining the worst thing that could ever happen to you. You are not protecting yourself by not believing in love and goodness. You are actually causing yourself to stay in the stuck place and the lost place. You are actually keeping yourself small.

God wants you to be big. God wants you to live your most clear and beautiful life. God wants you to be happy, and God wants you to fulfill your purpose and do what is yours to do. It doesn't help anyone when we stay small and broken. What will heal the world is when each and every one of us uncovers our special light and starts living inside of it. We all play a part in this world, and we all have a responsibility to find out what that part is.

You have a choice. You can stay small and broken, and you can live in the fear of bad things happening to you, or you can choose to live with faith in God and goodness. If you choose faith, goodness will naturally follow. It doesn't mean it will all be easy. For a while, at least, when you are still covered in the murkiness, it might be hard. But it keeps getting better. When you have made a commitment to yourself and to God that you are going to honor your divine spark and do what is yours to do, you will be given opportunities to do so. It is up to you to recognize those opportunities and follow the voice of the quiet place inside you that always knows what is next.

It is up to you to find your faith. What do you believe in? I believe in music and love and dancing and trees and mountains. I believe in myself, and I believe in you. I believe in a God who is loving and kind and whom I can be myself with. And I believe that God is always supporting me in going toward the light. I had to go through really hard things to find my way to the place where the light is. It took me a long time to believe that God was on my side. But now I understand that time when I couldn't feel God's love as a necessary part of my journey. I had to go through hard things because I had to heal what was mine to heal. I had to be firmly placed on my path so I could go where I needed to go. Sometimes, that path seemed dark and scary. But I kept walking, and I came out of the dark and scary places and into the place where I can see the light. You can, too.

Your faith is as unique and special to you as your purpose and your magnificence. Uncover what you believe in, and honor it with all of your heart. Choose to believe in your own goodness and in the goodness of the world. It can feel hard to believe in the goodness of the world when such awful things happen. But focusing on the awful things doesn't take you where you need to go. Focusing on the darkness brings more darkness. Believing solely in darkness is exactly what keeps us from the light.

You have a light inside of you. Nothing and no one can take that away. You have an inner nature of hopefulness and joy. It's who you truly are. You are meant to believe in something bigger than yourself. You are meant to follow the path of goodness and light; we all are. We are all responsible for our own journey. Even if people say you are too positive or too innocent, as they tell me sometimes, you can choose to follow the light instead of the darkness. You can choose to keep moving away from fear and toward love.

Love is your birthright. It is why you are here. It is yours to give and yours to receive. Begin to open to your faith by opening your heart to love. Stand tall against the fear and the darkness. Remember that you are strong like the ocean. Remember that the ocean lives inside of you. You are and always have been a part of something bigger than yourself. Maybe you understood that more deeply than most when you went to the soul place. Maybe your heart is just waiting for you to claim your place in things. Maybe God is waiting for you to ask a question. Maybe all you need to do is ask the quiet place for help and believe in its answer.

The path is clear before you. Use your faith to walk down it. I promise that there will be something beautiful for you waiting along the way. Open your eyes and be ready to see it. It is yours.

A Space for Beauty and Grace—
Chapter 10—Faith Meditation

Lie down on your back in a comfortable position.

Close your eyes, and take a deep breath in.

Imagine that you are standing underneath a waterfall.

The water is warm and invigorating, and you are able to let it wash over your whole body.

Picture it cleansing you inside and out, starting with the top of your head and moving down through each body part until you reach the bottoms of your feet.

Ask the water to cleanse all fear and all pain that keeps you from feeling your faith.

Let the water take away everything that no longer serves you.

Ask it to remove anything that keeps you from your most clear and beautiful life.

Now step out of the waterfall, and walk to the rock next to the stream.

Climb up on the rock and let the warmth of the sun caress you and dry your hair and your skin.

The warmth of the sun is like your faith.

It holds you and brings you joy and comfort.

Allow yourself to really feel the support of the rock beneath you and the sunlight on your body.

Listen to the sound of the waterfall, and begin to notice the sounds of the forest around you.

This is your place.

You belong here.

Relax and know that you are safe and protected and supported.

Your fear and your pain have left you completely.

You are washed clean by the healing waters, and you are made whole by the rays of the sun.

Notice the gentle joy that lives in your quiet place.

This joy is your faith and your belief in goodness.

Hold that joy in a place where you can always find it.

Ask your faith to be with you through your days in a way that you can feel it in your heart.

Take a few deep breaths in, and return to the room.

Notice your body, and remember that your faith is now always available to you.

CHAPTER ELEVEN

The Pathway

You might be wondering where you are going to go in your life now that you have decided not to be broken anymore. I hope that, by now, you have a clear idea of your purpose or at least you have a place to begin. I know you have at least started to think differently about yourself and your life and have come to the understanding that the possibilities for you are much bigger than you ever allowed yourself to believe before.

When we have been to the places that are called mental illness, the world can often set us apart. We become identified as different from everyone around us. There are the normal people—and us. We are the broken ones, the lost ones, the crazy ones. Our pathway veered from what was ordinary, so somehow, we are seen as people set apart.

But we cannot continue to believe in our separateness and allow ourselves to be different in a broken way. We cannot continue to stay lost. We have work to do, and to do it, we need to put ourselves back in the place where our humanity holds us in common with the rest of the world. At the most basic level of our humanness and also at the level of our souls, those who experience mental illness and those who don't are all the same. We have the same hearts beating in our chests and the same yearnings for love and meaning. We have the same call to fulfill our unique purpose, and we have the same need to find our own path to God.

You are on the path to wholeness already. You have come a long way since you were lost in the place of being broken. If you have even begun just to touch your magnificence with your fingertips, you are too far along to ever go back. You don't have to go back to all of the old lost places. What you have to do is uncover what is yours to do and begin to do it.

You might have been lost when you began to read this book, or you might have been simply standing still and not moving. We are past that place now. We have started walking together. I have been right here beside you all along. There are others on the path. Many, many others. Those who have experienced what we have experienced and those who have held us when we couldn't hold ourselves. We can all begin to hold each other. We are all in this together.

I had a conversation with the family members of people who have been to the lost places, as I have, this past week. I was a little nervous being my real self with them and sharing my story honestly. When I tell my story, I talk about healing and how my journey into what is called mental illness was very spiritual for me. I am not sure that people who really believe that what I went through is a disease or a disorder will take that. But it is my truth. I am not even sure how you have taken the fact that I believe that you are a healer. But that is my truth, too. And I think you are ready to hear it. And I hope the world around us is ready to hear our truth as well.

The family members I talked to were so open and kind and compassionate that they expanded my heart even farther toward those of us who experience the lost places and also to the ones who try to hold us and bring us back into the normal world again. They really don't understand where we go, and they want so desperately for us to be okay. They want so much to help us. And yet, we have to be the ones to choose to be okay again. And we have to do it in a way that honors where we have been.

That is our path. Our path is to walk out of the lost places. Our path is to find the beauty and the magic that was with us when we went there and bring it back into the ordinary world. Our path is to be the healers we are and to leave the broken places behind us altogether. Our path is like the path of every other human being on the planet. Our path is to find our inner light and live from it at every moment. Our path is to heal ourselves so that we can be of service to others. Our path is to mend the broken hearts of the world, starting with our own.

Your path is your own, and only you can find it and walk down it. But it is also a path that is well-worn and beaten down by many footsteps. For thousands of years, we as humans have been walking toward our own magnificence. We each have always been seeking our true path in the world. Stop believing that you are so broken and powerless that you don't have a path like everyone else. You do have a path, and that path will lead you directly to the only place you need to go, which is to the very heart and truth of who you really are.

Walking down our unique path to our greatness is what we are all born to do. And now is the time in the world when we have all the support we need available to do it. The universe is supporting us in healing ourselves and our planet, every step of the way. You are not alone. Stop believing that you are lost and powerless. Stop giving in to the darkness and the fear. Choose to be in the light. Then choose to share your light with others.

Choose to begin walking down your path. You will find your way to where you belong.

You do belong in this world. You belong in a life that is full of beauty and purpose. You belong in a circle of love. Your heart is magnificent, and your beauty is like the moon and the stars together. You had to go out of the ordinary world for a time, but you can come back now. I know you had to go there because you did. It was yours to do when you went there. But you have come back from there, and you don't have to be lost anymore. You don't have to keep going back there. But you have to recognize yourself as one who goes there. And then you have to ground yourself in this world so you can find yourself again. There is beauty in this world that belongs to you. Decide to walk down your path so you can find it.

I really do believe in you. I have showed you my path out of the darkness and the lost places. First, I did everything I could simply not to go back to the place that was lost. I grounded myself fully in this world and stood as still as my tree in the park. Eventually, after I had been standing still long enough, I started walking. I chose not to be lost anymore, and in so doing, I was able to find myself. And I found myself because I made the decision that I would. No one decided for me. I made a conscious choice to follow my own path to myself. That was the true beginning.

I didn't find myself in one day. It took time. It took an openness and a curiosity and a willingness to learn. I have had to learn everything I can about myself. I have had to be willing to go to the next place before me, even when I haven't known where it would take me. I have had to trust in something bigger than myself. And I have had to be willing to stop hiding. I have had to allow myself to be seen.

In order to be seen, I have needed to face my fear that people won't understand me. I have been talking to you all along about things that most people haven't understood yet. I have had to have the courage to say what is mine to say.

The path to yourself is also your path to freedom. You can't be free without doing what is yours. You have a responsibility and a purpose that you actually have to honor in order to get what you want in your life. In honoring your purpose, you are walking directly into the light. When we are living from our purpose, our path becomes easier and clearer. Beauty begins to find us in unexpected ways.

I have noticed lately that my inner light has changed. When I was lost or standing still, I felt heavy and sad and bogged down by life. When I started walking, I began to feel an energy inside of myself that felt vibrant and alive. The more I let go of fear and went where I needed to go, the more alive I felt. The more conscious I was about caring for myself and choosing love, the more I felt energy opening to me. But now something else has begun to happen.

The energy has shifted from just aliveness to being truly happy. When I am quiet and noticing how I feel, I can feel this light inside of me that can only be described as joy. I have uncovered my true inner nature. I have finally found that it is true what the sages of the world say. Our true nature is joy.

Your path to wholeness is also your path to joy. See where you are right now. When you are quiet and able to just notice how you feel in your body, how do you feel? What is your resting state like when you are not talking or working or doing anything at all? What are you like on the inside?

If you are sad or heavy or just neutral, it doesn't mean that there is no hope for you. It just means that you have work to do.

It just means that you have more to uncover. It just means that the green shoots of your soul haven't had enough room to grow into the light yet.

Those green shoots will begin to emerge. When you start walking down your path to wholeness, you will find the way for yourself to be whole. I didn't begin to experience the energy of quiet joy as a resting place until recently. But it was soon after I started down my path to wholeness that I began to notice the feeling of aliveness where the feeling of heaviness used to be. And that was something beautiful and unexpected.

There are lots of beautiful and unexpected gifts for you on your path. There will be lovely sunsets and beautiful pinecones and unexpected friends who show up in front of you. One day, you will begin to notice what I noticed recently, that your inner spark is like the wind—it is always around you, gently caressing you with its breath. Your light really is inside of you, waiting to be noticed.

You are never alone on your path. Yet you are always stepping along the way with your own feet. You are inside of yourself in a way that no one else is, yet you can always reach out to be touched.

Let the universe touch you. Let yourself be held. Let the wind in your hair be a gift from God. Find the path that only you know how to find out of your own darkness, and let yourself see all of the others who are walking along beside you.

We all have to face the darkness. It is a part of the world. It is not the special purview of those who experience what is called mental illness. We have our own version. Everyone does. Don't keep setting yourself apart from the world. Find the road to the place where you can be fully inside of your own magnificence.

You are of this world. You are breath and blood and bone. And also you are of the light that is eternal and sacred. The path to wholeness honors each of these parts of us. Those of us who have had a window into the world of dreams while we were awake can become so focused on coming back to the world of breath and blood that we forget to honor what is in us that is sacred. And when the world does everything it can to pull us back from that other place, sometimes we can lose the support we need to be who we really are.

We are more than people who are ill or lost. Our path is just as important and sacred as any other path that any other person can take. People who don't experience what we have experienced don't have a superior path to us. They don't deserve more beauty or more light or more happiness than we do. They don't deserve to live from their purpose in a way that we are blocked from because of where we have been.

In claiming our true paths for ourselves, we have to honor where we have been as sacred. We have to honor ourselves as sacred. We are the light. Just like everyone else. You can heal your light. And you can hold close what you have been through without dismissing it and making it wrong. It is what it is. And it is yours. Maybe you don't like it or understand it. Maybe everyone has tried to convince you that it was meaningless. But it is still yours.

Your path to wholeness begins and ends with you. Since you are human, you have something to forgive, and you have something to let go of that is keeping you from your true self. I have had many such things. We all do. The world doesn't always treat us kindly. We are exposed in our lives to more than just love. We are exposed to meanness and smallness and other people's fear. We are exposed to the darkness inside and outside of us. We have to walk through it to get to where we need to go.

Your path to your truest self will ask you to forgive. It will ask you to tell yourself the truth. It will ask you to face the parts of you that feel ugly. It will ask you to find your own beauty even when it's hard. It will ask you to love yourself first, before you can love anyone else in the world. It will challenge you and push you and make you see what you don't want to see.

It will ask of you what my path has asked of me. It will ask you to stop hiding. It will ask you to choose love, even when fear feels more convenient. I know you can do everything that your path will ask of you. Your path won't ask you anything that is impossible for you to do.

Sometimes, I take a little feeling-sorry-for-myself break right in the middle of my path. I declare that I am not doing one more thing. I am not listening to God or telling the truth or thinking about how I can fulfill my purpose for one more minute. I say, maybe I won't write this book, maybe I won't have a hard conversation with my teenage son, maybe I won't do anything big ever again. Maybe I won't do one more thing to be my most clear and beautiful self. Maybe I will just stand still and be quiet and let everything happen without me. My pity party usually only lasts for a little while. It is actually very helpful to let that part of me have a voice sometimes. Then I usually take a nap or go for a walk or clean the bathtub or talk to a friend, and I am back, willing to move forward again.

Our journey together so far has been intense. I realize that. It takes a lot of hard work to find our most clear and beautiful selves under all the murkiness and to go to the place where we can live our most clear and beautiful lives. It takes courage and strength and perseverance and resilience. It takes time and dedication.

It's a good thing we already have all of those things inside of us. Good thing our map to our most clear and beautiful life is always available to us. Good thing we have lots of support and love surrounding us all the time, even when we can't see it or feel it.

I hope you have seen the opening in the woods where your path begins. I hope you have begun to walk down it. I hope that you have felt the support of the tall trees and the green moss and the busy squirrels and the whole forest rising up to meet you with every step you have taken. I know you will come to a clearing, and I hope you can see the deer frolicking in the meadow and the birds gathering twigs for their nests. I hope your path through the woods takes you beside a beautiful waterfall and that you lose yourself in the sound of its gushing path down the stream. I hope a silver fox crosses the path in front of you and pauses to look you in the eye before he disappears into the trees. I hope you come to the place at the top of the mountain where you can see all of the other lovely, blue mountains spread out before you and that the sky is turning purple and pink from the sun.

This is your waterfall, your mountain, your sunset, your sky. This is you. This is who you really are inside. You are the waterfall. You are the mountain. You are the sunset. You are the sky. You are everything and everyplace that is beautiful. You are as magnificent as the deer and the birds.

You are as sacred as every other light in the world, and your path is just as important and meaningful and full of power. Inside of you already lives your most clear and beautiful self. You hold the map to your path to wholeness in your feet and your heart. Just start moving. Your soul knows where you have always been meant to go. Follow your path into your own true light. It is and always has been waiting for you.

A Space for Beauty and Grace—
Chapter 11—Power Helper Meditation

Sit comfortably with your feet on the floor.

Take a deep breath in.

Notice the noises around you, and gently shift your attention away from them and into the quiet inside of you.

Take a moment to center yourself in the quiet place that lives in your heart.

You are going to find the power helper that supports you in fulfilling your purpose in the world.

Let your mind go completely blank.

Then ask your quiet place a question.

Who or what represents your power in the world?

Is it an animal? Is it a force of nature? Is it a place in the world? Is it a calling or a relationship?

Take the time to quietly let whatever comes to you settle into your consciousness.

Ask it if it has a message for you.

Ask it how it supports you in being your most powerful self.

Ask it to come to you in your life and support you in doing what is yours to do.

Ask it how you can honor it in the world.

Thank your power helper for its strength and beauty.

Tell it you will remember it and call on it in the times to come.

Take a deep breath, and come back to the room.

Sit quietly for a few minutes, and let what you have discovered sink in.

Begin to honor this representation of your power in your daily life.

CHAPTER TWELVE

The Dance

We have walked down the path long enough together that now we have arrived in a new place. You have come a long way from where you were before. But the path is still open before you. There is more for you to do. A lot more. Your gifts to the world are as necessary as the sun. You shine as a light that can be seen from all of the other planets. You truly are what I have been telling you all along. You are exquisitely, profoundly magnificent. It is an honor to share this path with you. You have many blessings to give and to receive.

So where do we go when we claim our lives back and choose every day to be the brilliant, whole people that we were born to be? Where does our path take us after we have walked everywhere we needed to go to be healed? You have walked to the top of the mountain. Where do you go from here?

I will tell you that I walked so far to come here to you that now my feet hurt. Literally. I have walked a long, long way. It has been magical and beautiful—and it has also been hard. But I did it. And you can, too. I am at a place where I am actually well. I feel calm and centered and joyful. My life is about what is right with me again, and I have come past the hardest place to come out of, which was when my life was about everything that was wrong.

My life is beautiful. I can truly say that. I still have to do the laundry and wash the dishes and get my car repaired, but those are things that I have plenty of energy for and actually now enjoy. I can tell you that I have arrived here because I know the work I did to get here. I know that it is mine.

I have come here by doing everything that I have been called to do to get here. I have made a choice, again and again, to move toward healing and wellness. I have had a lot of healing over the past twelve years, and now I experience true wellness. Now I can do even more of what is mine to do because I have let go of the parts of myself that were holding me back from being who I am truly meant to be.

I am not afraid of the hard parts of the path anymore. I trust myself, and I trust in something bigger than myself to support me. Getting here has taken a long time. The fear of the worst thing lingered around me for much longer than any other fear. But now I can actually trust God in my heart. I can allow myself to believe in goodness. I can let my heart be open and trusting and true to who I really am in my center.

So where do we go after we have come past the hard parts? Where is your path ultimately taking you? I believe your path is taking you to where mine has taken me. To beauty and joy.

I came to a place in my path at the top the mountain where I could see the view of the landscape laid out before me. And something surprising and wonderful happened after I walked long enough and far enough. I began to dance.

This is actually the truth of what happened in my life on a physical level. I began my path to wholeness by walking. I walked a long, long way for many years. Every afternoon after work, you could find me out in the neighborhood, walking up and down the hills. For hours and hours, I walked, over the course of several years, while I was also facing my fears and uncovering my light from the murkiness where it had been hiding. I walked so much that my feet hurt.

And then I began to dance. I had heard of something called Conscious Dance when I first started walking. I had a postcard about it on my refrigerator during all of the years when I was spending hours walking. It never felt like the right time to go. But then, after I had walked and walked, I knew it was time, and I went to a class. And it has transformed my life. Because now I don't have to walk alone anymore. I can dance with other people. I can dance with people who are committed to finding their light and learning how to do what is theirs to do in the world. We all come together every week to do this through dance. Now I have found this incredible gift that is so healing and joyful to me. After journeying alone for most of my life, I can dance with other people who are healers like me.

And I do love to dance. You have your version of what I am sharing with you about my path. Maybe your path isn't literally about walking and dancing, as mine has been. But there is something that will take you where you need to go. You have a way to heal and to be whole. I have showed you my way. I hope you have found something here that you can carry with you always. I hope you have had a window into your true self.

Your journey might have felt solitary, as mine has. Maybe you have had to do most of the hard work on yourself alone. But you can come to a place where you are in a community of others. You can come to a place, as I have, where the people around you are just like you. People who are full of care about living their most clear and beautiful lives.

Your most clear and beautiful life is calling to you right now. I went to a dance workshop over New Year's that was all about transforming my life into what it has always been meant to be. I walked over the threshold into my new life, fully supported by the dance community around me. This book you are reading is the catalyst for my new life. What is the catalyst for yours? What can you do that only you can give to the world? What does your most clear and beautiful life look like?

In my most clear and beautiful life, I have a loving partner whom I can sing with and laugh with and share with and grow with. I am the best mom I can be to my children, and we have an open line of communication, and they always know that they are wholly loved. I have a career that revolves around who I am in my most clear and beautiful self. I am able to share with others what I have learned on my journey in a way that lights them up and shows them who they truly are. I know my own light, and in knowing that, can illuminate it in others. I am able to travel to the beautiful, sacred places in the world. I go on long walks, do yoga often, and dance as much as I can. I have friends whom I love, and we support each other in our own paths to joy and wholeness. I enjoy the simple pleasures of life, like a cup of tea on a cloudy day and a hot bath after a day of dancing. These are my dreams for myself. And most of them have already come true in a small way. But I know that they can all come true in a big way, too. All I have to do is keep dancing.

This is my most clear and beautiful life. What is yours? Give yourself permission to imagine it. Give yourself permission to live it. Decide to be about what is right with you. You and I, we are the same. We have gone to a lot of the same places. I have been to the lost places just like you. We both have something necessary and brilliant to offer to the world. We both ache for beauty and love to gather around us and hold us all of the time.

You have seen my heart. I have showed you who I am in my most true self. Who can you show your light to? Who needs to see it first? After you have uncovered it from the murkiness, who needs to see how it shines? I have a dear friend who has helped me every step of the way in coming to you and showing you who I am so you can be who you are. And we call the ones who we need to share our light with our people. She has her people. I have mine. Who are yours?

There are people in the world who absolutely need to see your light. They need to know who you are so they can be who they are. It might be surprising to you just how many people are yours to touch. My people are expanding. For a while, I thought I only could touch those of us who have been to the lost places. But recently, I have seen that it goes farther than that. I can also touch the people who try to hold us safe when we go there. I have also seen that there are people at all places on the path that are mine. People who are still lost and people who are standing still and people who have already been past the place at the top of the mountain where they are healed.

Your most clear and beautiful life is calling to you. Stop and listen to it for a while. Take your time. Do the work you need to do on yourself and then let the magic happen. Let the universe rise up to meet you on your path. Feel the earth beneath your feet, and raise your arms to the sky above you. Let yourself be anchored by the trees.

Walk where you need to go with the knowledge that someday you will be able to stop walking and start dancing. And remember that there will be others dancing with you. You will not be dancing alone. All of your people are ready and waiting for you to come to the place where they can see you. And once they see you, your life will never be the same. You will no longer need to hide in the shadows. You will be able to share your heart with others as I have shared mine with you.

We are all in this together, and we all need you. I know that you have everything you need inside of you to step into your most clear and beautiful life. I know that you have a divine spark within you that is glorious and alive. I know that you can be well. I know that you are on the path to wholeness.

We have come so far together on this journey. Now that we are about to part, I want you to know something. I want you to know that I am out here in the world supporting you. I believe in you, and I know you will go everywhere you need to go. There are others supporting you, too. All of us who have been to the lost places are coming to the place where we can support each other. We are finding our light, and we are sharing our light, and we are doing what is ours to do.

Maybe at the beginning of this book you felt alone. Maybe you felt like the weight upon you was so heavy that you could never break free from it. I have felt that way before. But we are in a different time and place now. It doesn't have to be true anymore that those of us who have experienced what is called mental illness have to stay lost and broken. We can join together in being whole. I am one of your people. And I can see the truth of who you are.

Find the others. They are all around you. They already love you. They are already waiting for you to step into the light and stop hiding. The universe is ready for you to be who you are meant to be. It is time.

Start living your most clear and beautiful life today. At least in a small way. Put fresh flowers on your bureau. Light a candle to symbolize the light that is inside of you. Call a friend you haven't seen for a while who always leaves you feeling inspired, and ask him out for coffee. Share some part of yourself with the world that has always longed to be seen.

Start walking. Start singing. Start painting. Start dancing. You have too much to do to stay still anymore. I can't promise you that all of the hard parts are over. I can't say that you will never be hurt or afraid again. I can't say that your people will be with you tomorrow. But I can promise you that they will come.

There is a path for you. And that path is directly linked to your light. If you keep choosing the darkness, the darkness will keep holding you. The way to your light is love and faith and beauty. The way to your light is the quiet place inside of you that always has an answer. Cultivate your quiet place in a way that makes sense to you. It might be walking or praying or meditating or writing or drawing. It might be reaching out to the people in your life whom you have been lost from. You have your own way. You just need to trust yourself enough to find it.

Going to the quiet place inside of us can feel scary at first. But if we choose to honor it, we will be blessed. I have been blessed many times on my path. What started out as the worst, most devastating, most awful thing that I could have ever imagined happening to me in my life has turned into the greatest blessing of all.

It has brought me here to you. And for that, I am eternally thankful. I couldn't have come to my light if I had never experienced the darkness. I couldn't have come to the place where I know who I am if I hadn't lost myself completely. I couldn't experience the true freedom that I feel now if I hadn't known what it was like to feel utterly trapped and locked in.

I am not saying that the answer for us when we go to the places called mental illness is handcuffs and locked wards and forced treatment like I experienced. Being locked up showed me the preciousness of freedom, but I am certain there is a better way. I am certain there is a more gentle, more loving, more kind way to help us when we go to the places that pull us from the ordinary world. I am sure there is a way for us to be held that will keep us from having to ever be broken and lost. I am certain that, if enough of us get together and have a conversation about another way that honors us as the sacred healers that we are and holds us in the light even when we appear lost, we can find a new way together.

You probably have experienced a lot of trauma, as I have, because you weren't honored as sacred when you were experiencing that other place. It has taken me a long time to find myself again after that trauma. I know that most of us who go to the other places called mental illness have been deeply hurt by the world. But I have hope that we can change this for the people who come after us. I am hoping that we, as a community of healers, find a better way. It is up to us to see our sacred purpose and to join together in fulfilling it.

In fact, I know that is the work of many of you who are reading this. I know that your light will be the answer for all of us in finding a way that we are held as the sacred healers that we are instead of as the broken people. I know that each of you have a calling that is essential to the rest of us, and I know that you have begun the work of finding a path that we can all take to come into the light.

I have shared with you what I have learned so far on my journey. I know I have a lot more to learn, and I know that you will teach me. The most important things that I want you to know are that you are sacred, you are a healer, and you are magnificent and full of light. I went to the other places so that I could tell you that. And I learned how to come back so I could offer you a path so that you can come back, too.

I am going to let go of your hand now so that you can start walking where you need to go. But I want you to remember that I am still holding you. I know about your magnificence. I know about your light. I know that you hold something precious that is necessary for all of us. And I know that you are on the path to where you can know these things for yourself.

You are supported. Feel the trees and the ocean and the rocks and the hawks. Feel your people all around you who need you and who love you already. Feel the constant presence of your quiet place. Feel God in your heart, and feel your own beauty and your own light. Feel your breath and your blood and your bones holding you. You have everything you need, right now and always, to be who you truly are. You are, right now, inside your heart and your soul, already your most clear and beautiful self. You have work to do. And that work is yours. But you also have something else. You have your most clear and beautiful life to live where you wake up every morning with the intention to dance. You have the hot springs to visit and the whales to see from the prow of the boat. You have the dolphins to swim with and the fire to sit by. You have everything beautiful that is already yours. Most important, you have yourself.

You are sacred. You are beautiful. Your light is as brilliant as the North Star in the winter sky. I am honored to be on this journey with you. You have already given me more blessings than I can count. I honor you. And I wish you many blessings to come. Please do what is yours to do in the world. The rest of us need you. Don't be afraid of your magnificence anymore. Go ahead. Let your light shine.

A Space for Beauty and Grace—
Chapter 12—The Dance Meditation

Go to the most beautiful place in your home.

Sit or lie quietly in a space that you have created that makes your heart sing because it is so beautiful to you.

Look around at the beauty you have created.

If you have a candle, sit it beside you and light it with a gentle prayer to God to watch over you and hold you in the light.

Now close your eyes.

Take a deep breath in.

Put your hands over your heart where the quiet place lives.

Ask the quiet place what is yours to do now that you have found yourself again.

After you have done all of the hard work and have walked as far through the fear and the uncertainty and the darkness as you have needed to, what is yours to do in the light?

What does the light look like for you?

Who is there to share it with you?

What beauty awaits you that you will wake up to every morning and delight in all day long?

What sacred beauty is yours to hold?

Take a moment to honor where you have been.

Thank your feet for carrying you down your long path.

Make a commitment to honor what is yours still to do.

Make a commitment to surround yourself in beauty and to honor the light inside of you.

Choose now to follow your own path into the magnificence of your soul.

Give thanks for all you have learned and for everything that has brought you to this moment.

Take a deep breath in, and remember who you are.

Open your eyes, and see the beauty in front of you.

You own it.

It's yours.

CONCLUSION

We have come a long way together. And I know we each have yet farther to go. I hope that, by now, your life is more supported, more beautiful, more purposeful, and more reflective of the brilliance that is truly you. I am honored that you have come this far with me. And now I am going to ask you a favor. Stop being broken, and start living from the truth of who you are. You already know all about the broken places. You have been lost everywhere that you needed to be lost. You deserve more now. You deserve comfort and beauty and joy. You deserve a dancing partner and feather-light feet and a room full of flowers and your favorite music pulsing through the air around you. For so long, those of us called mentally ill have been living in the place of not enough. Not enough love, not enough joy, not enough purpose, not enough support, not enough beauty. It is time for us to let our hearts be full of light and color. If you still get lost sometimes, it's okay. But make a commitment to yourself that you will stay in the lost places for less time. Make an agreement with your heart that you will learn everything you need to from the hard places so that it doesn't have to keep being hard. The whole world is waiting for you to exhale so it can take in its own breath. Take your own heart into your hands, and do it. Breathe. Live. Love. Celebrate. Dance. You have come so far. You have walked bravely through the hard and scary places. But you can see that there is more for you. Reach out your hand to touch it.

Pull it close to you. You are enough. More than enough. Believe in yourself, and do what is yours to do. I will be there with you. And so will the whole beautiful world. Thank you for being who you are. Thank you for your courage to be even more of yourself. Thank you for your willingness to go to the quiet place that lives inside of you. That is your place. It will always show you what is next. And what is next right now is you. Amazing, brilliant, magnificent you. It is my honor to share this journey with you. I will always keep you in my heart. Thank you for your beauty. You have touched my soul.

ABOUT THE AUTHOR

Beth Gager has a master's degree in counseling from the College of William and Mary and has worked in the mental health field for many years. Her inspiration for this book comes from the hardest thing she has had to do so far in her life, which is to go to the places that our world calls mental illness. She has been inspired by the many beautiful people she has met who have been called to walk a similar path. She is grateful that she has found a way to come back from that place where she appeared to be lost. Her life purpose is to share the amazing beauty and grace she has found on her journey out of the hard places and into the joyful places. Her message is for others like her who want to walk out of the dark, tangled woods where they have been trapped and find their way into the bright, green meadows that are calling to them from the quiet places that live inside their hearts. She loves to walk, write, and dance and longs to sing with the guitar. She lives with her two children in the mountains in Charlottesville, Virginia.

Made in the USA
Middletown, DE
14 November 2016